FACTORY LEGISLATION IN INDIA

By the same author

I. Factory Labor in India

A critical and analytical study in the rise, growth, conditions and problems of the factory workers in India.

II. Hindustani Workers on the Pacific Coast

A study in the social and economic conditions of the Hindustanees on the Pacific Coast, based on the report made by the author as special agent to the Department of Labor, United States Government.

III. The Labor Movement in India

A critical and analytical study in the working class movement in India with special reference to its origin, development, nature and significance.

Printed in Germany.

FACTORY LEGISLATION IN INDIA

By

Rajani Kanta Das, M. Sc., Ph. D.

Late Lecturer in Economics, New York University;
Former Special Agent, United States Department of Labor.

With an Introduction

By

John R. Commons, M. A., LL. D.

Professor of Economics, University of Wisconsin;
Former Member Industrial Commission of Wisconsin and
United States Commission on Industrial Relations.

1 9 2 3

WALTER DE GRUYTER & Co.

VORMALS G. J. GÖSCHEN'SCHE VERLAGSHANDLUNG —
J. GUTTENTAG, VERLAGSBUCHHANDLUNG — GEORG
REIMER — KARL J. TRÜBNER — VEIT & COMP.

BERLIN and LEIPZIG

TO MY MOTHER

INTRODUCTION.

By Dr. John R. Commons.

Mr. Das came to the investigation of Indian factory legislation as a part of several years' investigation of the forces that make for national efficiency. Deeply impressed by the famine reports of 1900—01 and the abject poverty of the people of India, he devoted himself to the improvement of economic conditions by prolonged study of the causes. Seeing that the majority of the people of India depended upon agriculture for a living, he came to America to prepare himself for the study of agricultural production. While pursuing these studies at Ohio State University, the University of Missouri and the University of Wisconsin, it became clear to him that national prosperity depended more upon the industrial efficiency of the people than upon the natural resources of the country. The real cause of India's poverty was her industrial inefficiency. The solution lay in becoming industrially efficient.

This conclusion led Mr. Das to the study of the human element in the production system — the labor problem. This he followed at the University of Chicago and the University of Wisconsin, working betimes in American factories as an employee, and travelling extensively in England, France, and the United States, besides in India on a return visit.

This unusually extensive preparation for the study of Indian factory legislation, has given to the book an unusual value, not only as a study of a single country, but especially by way of the comparative legislation and actual factory practice which he has had always before him.

It is difficult for a Westerner to appreciate and weigh all of the facts which Mr. Das has marshalled in this important study of Indian industry, but certainly at no time in history is it more necessary to do so. For India is nearer to us than before, and the problems of the British Empire are becoming the problems of America. To the understanding of these economic, political and legislative problems this book is a valuable contribution.

University of Wisconsin. John R. Commons.

PREFACE.

"Factory Legislation in India" is a study in the legislative institution relating to Indian factories with special reference to the social, political and economic forces which led to its origin and growth and influenced its nature and function. Originally, it constituted only a chapter of the treatise on factory labor in India in 1913 and was elaborated into the present treatise in 1916 as a dissertation for the degree of Doctor of Philosophy at the University of Wisconsin. Except for the addition of a chapter on the Factory Act of 1922 and for a few other minor additions and alterations, the present treatise is practically the same as the original dissertation of 1916. A summary of the first three legislations was published in the Modern Review, Calcutta, January, 1921.

In presenting the treatise to the public, the author is conscious that it is far from being exhaustive. Some of the Indian documents, periodicals and newspapers, which could very profitably have been consulted, were not available in this country. There was, however, full access to the most important sources of information on the subject, namely, the British Parliamentary Papers and Debates, the Proceedings of the Indian Legislative Council and the Debates of the Legislative Assembly and of the Council of State of India, and a complete file of the London Times. Moreover, since the main object of the investigation was not so much the collection of the detailed information on the history of factory legislation as the analysis of the underlying forces, the author is satisfied that although a few details might have been added and some of the points elaborated, they would not have made any essential difference in the fundamental character of the treatise.

In conclusion, the author takes this opportunity to express his deep gratitute to Dr. John R. Commons, Professor of Economics, University of Wisconsin, who has, as his teacher, not only supervised the preparation of the treatise, but has also generously written an introduction to it. He is also indebted to Mr. Jay Bowman, Chicago, Ill., and to Mrs. Victoria B. Turner of the Bureau of Labor Statistics, for reading the manuscript and offering valuable criticisms. He also takes this occasion to express his thanks to the Library of the University of Wisconsin and the Economics Division of the New York Public Library for assistance in locating and collecting some of the documents consulted in the preparation of this volume.

New York, August 1, 1922. Rajani Kanta Das.

DOCUMENTARY BIBLIOGRAPHY.

Full Names and Abbreviations of the References.

A. Publications of the British Parliament.

Gt. Brit. Parl. Papers — 1876, Vol. 56, H. of C. 56.	Correspondence relative to the Indian Tariff Act of 1875.
— 1876, Vol. 56, C. 1515.	Further Correspondence.
— 1876, Vol. 56, H. of C. 219.	Financial Dispatch, No. 364, of 15th July, 1875, relating to the Tariff Act of India.
— 1888, Vol. 77, H. of C. 321.	Report on Bombay Factory Commission, dated 6th January, 1885, and on the Resolution of the Government of Bombay.
— 1889, Vol. 58, H. of C. 124.	Reports on the Workings of the Indian Factory Act made to the Government of India in reply to the Inquiries by the Secretary of the State for India.
— 1889, Vol. 58, H. of C. 162.	Report on further Correspondence relating to the Amendment of the Indian Factory Act of 1881.
— 1890—91, Vol. 59, H. of C. 86.	Report on the recent Commission on Indian Factories, 1890—91.
— 1890, Vol. 81, C. 5914.	Correspondence respecting the proposed International Labor Conference at Berlin.
— 1890, Vol. 81, C. 6042.	Further Correspondence respecting the International Labor Conference at Berlin. In continuation of C. 5914.
— 1890, Vol. 59, H. of C. 194.	An Act to amend the Indian Factory Act of 1881, being an Act No. XI. of 1891, of the Governor General in Council.
— 1890—81, Vol. 59, H. of C. 120.	Dispatches from the Secretary of State to Indian Government dated 13th May and 3rd July, 1891, relating to the Amendment of the Indian Factory Act of 1881.
— 1890—91, Vol. 59, H. of C. 224.	Return of Further Correspondence relating to the Amendment of the Indian Factory Act of 1881 by the Indian Factory Act of 1891.

— 1892, Vol. 36, C. 6795—IX.	Royal Commission on Labor. Report on the Labor Question in India.
— 1893—94, Vol. 65, H. of C. 151.	Indian Factory Act Regulations under the Factory Act of 1891.
— 1894, Vol. 58, H. of C. 108.	Correspondence with the Government of India on the subject of Inspection of Factories and of the Factory Inspectors.
— 1907, Vol. 59, Cd. 3617.	Report of the Indian Textile Factory Labor Committee of 1906.
— 1908, Vol. 74, Cd. 4292.	Report of the Indian Factory Labor Commission of 1907. Vol. I. Report and Appendices.
— 1909, Vol. 63, Cd. 4519.	The same. Vol. II. Evidence.
— 1873, Vol. 59, H. of C. 172. and so on	Statement Exhibiting the Moral and Material Progress and Condition of India from 1871 on.
— 1875, Vol. 16, C. 1184. and so on	Reports of the Inspectors of Factories and Workshops in Great Britain.
— 1904, Vol. 102, Cd. 1801. and so on	Statistical Abstracts relating to British India.
— 1920, Cmd. 627.	Draft Conventions and Recommendations adopted by International Labor Conference at its first annual meeting at Washington, D.C. 1919.
Parliamentary Debates.	Hansord's Parliamentary Debates, up to 1892, and Parliamentary Debates from 1893 on. Parliamentary Debats, House of Commons, 1909 on.

B. Publications of the Government of India and of the Local Governments.

Act No. XV of 1881.	A Collection of Acts passed by the Governor General of India in Council in 1881.
Act No. XI of 1891.	A Collection of Acts passed by the Governor General of India in Council in 1891.
Act No. XII of 1911,	A Collection of Acts passed by the Governor General of India in Council in 1911.
Bombay Factory Commission.	Report of the Commissioners appointed on March 23, 1875, by the Government of Bombay to inquire into the conditions of the operatives in the Bombay factories and the necessity for the passing of a factory act.

Bombay Factory Report.	Annual Factory Report of the Presidency of Bombay. From 1900 on.
C. P. & Berar Factory Report.	Resolutions on the Working of the Indian Factories Act in Central Provinces and Berar from 1900 on.
Hyderabad Factory Report.	Report on the Working of the Indian Factories Act in Hyderabad and Assigned Districts from 1900 on.
Indian Legislative Council.	Abstracts of the Proceedings of the Council of the Governor General of India assembled for the purpose of makking Laws and Regulations.
Indian Legislative Council	Proceedings of the Council of the Governor General of India assembled for the purpose of making Laws and Regulations.
Punjab Factory Report.	Report on Working of the Indian Factories Act in the Punjab, from 1900 on.
	Statistics of British India.
	Legislative Assembly Debates.
	Council of State Debates.

CONTENTS.

CHAPTER I.

INTRODUCTION.

An institution is a means through which social life finds specific expression. Since an institution arises out of the need for such expression, new institutions appear whenever social, political and economic forces bring about a situation requiring a new expression or direction of social life. The application of mechanical power in production revolutionised the industrial organisation and gave rise to the factory system. The institution of factory legislation appeared primarily in response to the social condition of the people under the present system of production and so came to form an integral part of the modern industrial society.

The prime object of factory legislation is the amelioration of some of the conditions affecting injuriously the workers under the factory system. Changes in the productive technique, such as the use of machinery and of mechanical power and the employment of a large number of people in a certain time and place, have subjected the workers to the dangers of disease and accident and created other similar problems. It has, therefore, become the function of the State through its legislative and administrative organs to regulate some of these conditions in the interest of public health and morals.

The origin and growth of factory legislation has been subjected to the influences of various forces arising from conflicting interests. The first and foremost of these conflicts is that between labor and capital. The chief purpose of a business enterprise under the modern system of production is to make profit. Any change or improvement in the conditions of employment, such as shorter hours of work or accident compensation, if it tends to decrease profits, is inevitably opposed by capitalistic interests. The laborer, on the other hand, under the present wage system, is not interested in working longer or producing more than what is absolutely necessary to insure himself a living wage, while leaving the employer a profit just sufficient to induce him to continue in business. The demands of labor are, therefore, sometimes higher than business conditions warrant.

The progress of labor legislation is also affected by the conflicting interests of conservatives and reactionaries on the one hand, and of reformers and "uplifters' on the other. The former have been accustomed to existing institutions or are direct or indirect beneficiaries of modern economic organization. They resist, therefore, any innovation or restrictive measures on the privileges of the capitalists or of their own. As some of them wield great political power, they exert an important influence on labor legislation. The latter, on the other hand, are inspired by the conception of a new order of society to be achieved, in part, by bettering the conditions of labor, or with the vision of a millennium to result from the emancipation of the masses. They have, therefore, espoused the cause of labor and demanded progressive legislation.

There is still another set of forces which have a bearing upon factory legislation. In enacting restrictive measures, such as those related to child and woman labor, legislators have always taken international competition into consideration. Commercial rivalry has been a detriment to the achievement of progressive labor laws in many countries. On the other hand, the common understandings and agreements arrived at in the international conferences, such as those at Berlin and Berne, and especially those lately inaugurated under the auspices of the International Labor Office of the League of Nations, have promoted the standardisation of the labor laws of different countries.

In addition to the above forces more or less common to all countries, the problem of factory legislation in India is complicated by several special factors. India's political and economic dependence upon Great Britain has given rise to conflicting forces in so far as factory laws are concerned. The manufacturing and commercial interests of Great Britain look upon India as a market where they can buy and sell at their pleasure. They do not look with favor upon the growth of manufacturing in India, and insist that the British factory laws be applied to Indian factories. The British capitalists, on the other hand, who have invested money and started factories in India, regard domestic British manufacturers as rivals and resent any interference by the latter with manufacturing industries and labor legislation in India. As the interest of the Indian capitalists is the same as that of the British capitalists with investments in India, the former always side with the latter. The pride and patriotism of the Indian public are also wounded by outside interference with affairs over which it thinks it is entitled to having exclusive control. It protests, therefore, against outside interference.

How these divergent forces arising from conflicting interests led to the origin and growth, and determined the nature and function of factory legislation in India, is the subject matter of this treatise.

CHAPTER II.

FACTORY ACT OF 1881.[1]

Rise of the Cotton Industry.

The first steam power factory in Bombay was started in 1863. In 1871—72 there were no less than 11 spinning and weaving companies in that city, working 404,000 spindles and 4,294 looms by means of 19 steam engines. There were also 3 such factories in other towns of the Presidency.[2] In 1872—73 the 18 cotton factories of Bombay, Kurla, Broach, Surat and Ahmedabad, were found to employ 10,000 laborers and to turn out 100,000 lbs. of yarn daily.[3] The following year there was a still more rapid increase. No less than 9 jointstock companies were registered during the period and the value of the exported cotton piece goods from Bombay increased from £ 191,336 to £ 254,571.[4] The number of factories in the city of Bombay alone increased to 28, while those in the interior of the Presidency to 8. The importation of heavier and coarser kinds of cotton goods practically stopped, while on the other hand, the Indian cotton products found a ready sale in Russia, America, and China.[5]

While Bombay was taking such rapid strides in her manufacturing career, Bengal was not far behind. During the same decade, along the banks of the Hooghly, below and above Calcutta, 15 great factories for the spinning and weaving of cotton and jute arose. In the meantime the importation of machinery into India was also increasing rapidly. In 1870 India imported from England

---

[1] This act is officially called the "Factories" Act. But it has also been referred to as the Factory Act. The latter designation seems to the author to be more appropriate and has been used throughout the book.

[2] Gt. Brit. Parl. Papers, 1873, Vol. 50, H. of C. 172, p. 92.

[3] Ibid., 1874, Vol. 49, H. of C. 196, p. 109.

[4] Ibid., 1875, Vol. 54, H. of C. 406, p. 16.

[5] Ibid., 1876, Vol. 56, H. of C. 406, p. 49.

machinery to the value of £ 300,000, while the value of the machinery so imported in 1875 was £ 1,500,000.[6]

Agitation in England for Regulating Indian Factories.

This phenomenal growth of Indian manufacturing industries could not long continue without eliciting the notice and protest of the British commercial interests, which had the privilege of an almost unrivalled market in India. Considerable apprehension was in fact felt in England, when the *Statement exhibiting the moral and material progress and condition of India during* 1872—1873 announced, in 1874, the existence of 18 cotton factories in the midst of the cotton growing regions of India and added that the weekly consumption of cotton was 1,500 bales, or only 6.5 per cent of the average cotton crop of the country and that this was likely to increase rapidly. It was also remarked that many cotton printers had settled in Bombay and much of the cotton manufactured in the factories was dyed in the vicinity[7]. On August 7, 1874, there was an article in the London *Times*[8] from its own correspondent, who gave a glowing description of the rise of steam-power factories near Calcutta, and remarked that ghauts, wharves, jetties, warehouses, and embankments were fast making the left bank of the Hooghly at Calcutta another Liverpool. "The spirit of manufacturing enterprise," added the correspondent, "has a very important bearing on our native subjects. If, in Bengal, at least, they do not yet supply the capital or start new projects, the upper classes must in time learn the advantages of associated labor in the production of manufactures".[9]

About this time Major Moore, inspector-in-chief of the cotton department in Bombay, stated in his report that

[6] Gt. Brit. Parliamentary Debates, 1877, 235 : 1091. According to Mr. Jackson of Blackburn, in 5 years ending in 1874 England exported 60 per cent less cotton goods into India than she did in 5 years ending in 1856.

[7] Gt. Brit Parl. Papers, 1874, Vol. 49, H. of C. 196, p. 109.

[8] *Ibid.*, p. 3, c. 3.

[9] *Loc. cit.*, p. 3, c. 3.

the Bombay mills employed a large number of women and children, who derived great benefit from the work, but that the advantage carried with it a corresponding disadvantage: the working time was long; the labor fatiguing; and the weekly day of rest, lacking. In his opinion, it was useless to expect that women and children in Indian factories would be shown a consideration greater than that accorded to similar classes of employees in English factories prior to government regulation.[10] In his report on British factories for the half year ending October 31, 1874, Mr. Alexander Redgrave, inspector of factories, referred to the rapid growth of cotton factories in India and pointed out the necessity for factory regulation, due to the fact that a large number of children was employed in them. "It is clear, therefore, concluded Mr. Redgrave, "that this is a progressive industry, and looking to what factory legislation has achieved in this country, may we not hope that the native workers of India may be spared the ordeal which our cotton operatives went through in former days, and that they may be permitted to enjoy the blessings of moderate labor, of ample time for rest and meals, and of protection to children of tender age".[11]

One of the results of the publication of the statistics regarding textile industries in India was that they gave rise to general discussion among the British public. On May 7, 1875, one Mr. Helms read a paper on "The Growth of the Factory System of India" at the Society of Arts rooms in London. In the discussion which followed the reading of the paper, Mr. Hugh Mason argued, apparently with convincing reasons, that India was destined to become a great manufacturing country. He admitted that India had disadvantages, but asserted that they would soon be overcome. First, the efficiency of the employee would gradually increase, as had been the case in other countries. Second, the Indian manufacturer with the growth of competition would buy machinery as cheaply

[10] Gt. Brit. Parliamentary Debates, 1875, 222 : 76. India, Legislative Council Proceedings, Calcutta, 1879, 18 : 239—40.

[11] Gt. Brit. Parl. Papers, 1875, Vol. 16, C. 1184, p. 30.

as did the English operator. Third, the quality of Indian cotton had been improving and Egyptian cotton would also be delivered as cheaply at Bombay as at Liverpool. India, moreover, had a certain advantage over England. Due to the proximity of the cotton growing regions, Indian factories could use unpressed cotton, which could be spun several hanks finer per pound than the pressed cotton of the same quality. If the reported discovery of coal suitable for steam were real, he added, there was nothing wanting in order that India might successfully compete with English manufacturers.[12]

In the Times of the same issue, a writer pointed out that nothing short of choking down the rising manufacturing industry of India by a prohibitive excise duty, could possibly arrest its natural growth. Whatever might be the difference of wages between the two countries, India, with a population of 250,000,000 would successfully compete with England, which had a population of only 30,000,000. "In conclusion, let me add", continued the writer, "that English and also European manufacturers must similarly be affected by the competition with the cheap labor of the East; and, unless some unlooked-for convulsions should arise, it is plain that all the wool of the Cape and our Australian Colonies will one day be made up in India for exportation to Europe."[13]

The most important effect of the reports on the growth of the cotton industry in India was, however, the rise of the spirit of rivalry among Lancashire manufacturers, who were afraid of losing their market in India, where they sent about one-fourth of their annual export.[14] They, therefore, started a strong agitation. Their immediate object was twofold: First, they intended to have the Indian market free from any import duty on their goods, whether fiscal or protective. Second, they intended to apply the British factory law to India, so that their competitors, some of whom were English capitalists, could not enjoy any "un-

[12] The Times, London, Sept. 22, 1875, p. 6, c. 4.
[13] Ibid.
[14] Gt. Brit. Parliamentary Debates, 1877, 235 : 1091.

due" privilege over them. The agitation was taken up by their representatives, both in and out of Parliament. The press and the philanthropists also joined the clamor for reform.

The first and most effective attack was made on the revenue duty, which in India was imposed on all importations, including cotton goods. The duty was rather insignificant and had existed even under the rule of the East India Company at the rate of 5 per cent *ad valorem*. This rate was, however, raised to 10 per cent after the Indian Mutiny of 1857, but was reduced again to 7.5 per cent in 1864. Lancashire manufacturers had already made several attempts, not altogether without success, to abolish or at least to materially reduce the duty on the importation of their cotton goods into India.

Early in January of the year 1874, Mr. Fairweather, Ancoats, Manchester, wrote to the Premier showing the effect of a 5 per cent duty on Manchester goods imported into India. A manufacturer in Lancashire, for instance, investing £ 88,000 in a cotton mill and producing £ 140,000 worth of cotton goods per annum had to pay £ 7,000 as duty, or 8 per cent on his capital invested. Mr. Fairweather contended that this iniquity needed a speedy remedy at the hands of her Majesty's Government. As an excise duty on manufactures might be resented by employers in India, he suggested the introduction of a license system, by which a manufacturer in India would have to pay a tax of 3 shillings per spindle and 21 shillings per loom before he could start a cotton textile factory. In reply Mr. Fairweather received the following note from her Majesty's Government: "Mr. Gladstone will communicate with the Secretary of State for India on the subject".[15]

About this time a deputation from the Manchester Chamber of Commerce was also sent to Lord Salisbury, Secretary of State for India, to urge the abolition of the duty on their cotton goods imported into India. The

[15] The *Times*, London, Jan. 5, 1874, p. 11, c. 4.

deputation stated that Indian manufacturers were rapidly increasing the number of their factories, that they could also import, free from duty, Egyptian and American cotton, and thus compete with Lancashire manufacturers in the production of finer goods; and that it would, therefore, be expedient, in the interest of Indian consumers and in justice to English manufacturers, to remove the import duty levied by the India Government.[16]

Having promised the Lancashire people what they wanted,[17] Lord Salisbury, in his dispatches, first on March 26, and then on October 28, 1874, advised Lord Northbrook, Governor General of India, to consider the representation of the Manchester Chamber of Commerce. In the meantime, he also took up the question of factory legislation and, on April 30, 1874, commended the subject to the best attention of the Government of Bombay. Shortlv before this time he had received an unofficial representation regarding the evil effects of the system of work that was in force in Bombay factories.[18]

The discussion on the necessity of factory legislation for India was first opened in the House of Commons on Feb. 8, 1875, when Mr. Anderson, Glasgow, asked the Under Secretary of State for India whether he was aware that an extensive factory system was growing up in India without any Government supervision for the protection and health of the women and children employed and whether the Indian Government would adopt some such factory legislation as then prevailed in Great Britain for the prevention of such evils before they had attained greater proportion.[19]

In the same month, the Secretary of State, whose attention had also been drawn by Miss Carpenter, the well-known English philanthropist in India, to the prevalence of long hours of work in Indian factories, again directed an inquiry for the purpose of ascertaining

[16] Gt. Brit. Parl. Papers, 1876, Vol. 56 C. 1515, p. 4.

[17] Gt. Brit. Parliamentary Debates, 1876, 227 : 1951.

[18] Ibid., 1875, 222 : 76.

[19] Ibid.

whether any cause for legislation existed and, if so, what course might be adopted.[20]

The question of repealing the import duty was renewed in the House of Commons by Mr. J. K. Cross, Bolton, who on March 9, 1875, asked the Under Secretary of State for India whether there was any probability for an early abolition of the protective duties then imposed by the Indian Government upon the importation of cotton goods; if not, whether there would be any material reduction of them. In reply, the Under Secretary said that the subject of import duties, especially of those referred to, was under consideration by a tariff committee then sitting in India. The Under Secretary pointed out, at the same time, that these duties were imposed for revenue purposes, and could not correctly be called "protective".[21]

About this time the Tariff Committee appointed by the Governor General finished its investigation. The Indian Government could not spare the amount of revenue derived from the duty on cotton goods and any substitute was found to be objectionable. On March 13, 1875, the committee submitted its report recommending the retention of the import duty on Manchester goods.[22]

With reference to this decision, the Secretary of State pointed out, in his dispatch of July 15, 1875, to the Government of India, that the duty on imported cotton goods was not oppressive, though it might act as a protection, but it was objectionable on political grounds. The gradual transfer of the Indian trade from the English to the Indian manufacturer, which appeared likely to happen, would make the interests of England antagonistic to those of India, and create a feeling of animosity on each side. It should, therefore, be repealed at the earliest possible time.[23]

The problem of legislation for Indian factories was soon taken up in the House of Lords by the Earl of Shaftsbury, the well-known philanthropist and undaunted

---

[20] Gt. Brit. Parliamentary Debates, 1875, 226 : 212.
[21] Ibid., 222 : 1484—85.
[22] The Times, London, March 13, 1875, p. 5, c. 2.
[23] Gt. Brit. Parl. Papers, 1876, Vol. 56, H. of C. 56, pp. 3—4.

champion of factory legislation for over forty years. On July 30, 1875, Lord Shaftsbury drew the attention of their lordships to Mr. Redgrave's remark on Indian textile industry, noted above, and described how rapidly it was growing. Pointing out the necessity of regulating labor in factories, he urged that factory laborers in India be saved, while the industry was still young, from the difficulties and complications to which British laborers had been subjected in the past. "There is also a commercial view to this question", continued Lord Shaftsbury, "we must bear in mind that India has raw material and cheap labor; if we allow the manufacturers there to work their operatives for 16 or 17 hours and put them under no restrictions, we are giving them a very unfair advantage over the manufacturers of our own country, and we might be undersold even in Manchester itself by manufactured goods imported from the East".[24]

In reply, Lord Salisbury expressed his satisfaction that the noble lord, whose philanthropy was above suspicion, had taken up the cause of Indian factory laborers. The proposal to limit the hours of labor in India, he said, was looked upon as a great conspiracy for the purpose of promoting British manufactures and of stifling Indian manufactures under the guise of philanthropy. Referring to the future of cotton manufacture in India, which he thought, was very bright due to the natural advantages, and referring also to the great prejudice of the Indian people against any reform, the Secretary of State assured their lordships that in spite of all obstacles, the Government of India would show no shortcoming in the discharge of its high duties and would do its best to apply to the people of India the legislation which had been so beneficial to England.[25]

Meanwhile the proposal of Lord Salisbury for the repeal of the import duty was again under consideration by the Government of India. But no way was found to give effect to it. Finally, it was decided that there should

[24] Gt. Brit. Parliamentary Debates, 1875, 226 : 211.

[25] Ibid., pp. 213—14.

be some reduction of the duty, and on August 5, 1875, a new Tariff Act was passed at Simla. It was signed by the Governor General and became effective on the same day. By its provision the general rate of 7.5 per cent *ad valorem* on imports was reduced to 5 per cent. The tariff valuation on cotton goods was lowered to an extent which incurred to the Government of India, a loss of revenue amounting to £ 88,000 per annum. On the other hand, a duty of 5 per cent was also imposed on long staple raw cotton imported into India.[26]

The act did not meet the approval of Lord Salisbury, as it did not give any assurance that the import duty would be repealed in a definite period of time. In connection with this act, the India Government also violated the established principle that the Secretary of State should be kept in touch with the nature of all important measures brought before the Indian Legislative Council. In a dispatch on November 11, 1875, he strongly attacked the provision of the act imposing 5 per cent import duty on long staple raw cotton. It was undoubtedly intended as a protection to the English industry against competition in the finer articles of manufacture, but the effect of this duty might be to retard, and even perhaps, to prevent, the growth of an important branch of Indian industry and he was, therefore, unable to sanction it. Referring to his dispatch of July 15, 1875, Lord Salisbury again pointed out the importance of repealing the import duty for political reasons and showed that it was also wrong economically, as it offered a false encouragement to Indian manufacturers, which tended to divert them from the effort by which alone their success could be permanently secured. "The entire removal of the duty should, however," concluded Lord Salisbury, "not be adjourned for an indefinite period, but the provision should be made for it within a fixed term of years".[27]

The demand of the Secretary of State on the Government of India that the import duty on cotton goods should

---

[26] The *Times*, London, Sept. 6, 1875, p. 10, c. 1.

[27] Gt. Brit. Parl. Papers, 1876, Vol. 56, H. of C. 56, pp. 69—71.

be repealed at the instigation of Manchester manufacturers, aroused discussion and criticism both in India and in England. The Indian press strongly criticised Lord Salisbury's policy. Mr. J. M. MacLean, later on an advocate of the Lancashire interests in the House of Commons, wrote, on Feb. 28, 1876, in the Bombay Gazette, of which he was then the editor, as follows: — "Give Manchester what she wants or go — that is what Lord Salisbury demanded of the Viceroy. What can be more scandalous, to avail ourselves of Lord Salisbury's own words, than for an English Minister deliberately to sell India to Manchester? Yet this is what the Secretary of State proposed to do. In return for the support given by Lancashire to the conservatives at the last election, and with an eye to the future favors of the same kind, Lord Salisbury intends to deprive India of a revenue of three-quarters of a million sterling a year, to make a present of it, in the first instance at all events, to the English manufacturer of cotton goods".[28]

But the real test for Lord Salisbury came in the House of Commons on March 14, 1876, when Viscount Halifax, a former Secretary of State for India, severely criticised his insistence on the repeal of the import duty in spite of the India Government's inability to do so, and especially his conduct towards Lord Northbrook in this connection.[29] In reply, Lord Salisbury reiterated the reasons for the policy given in his dispatches quoted above, and said that he would not consent to look upon Lancashire interests with contempt. But he added, it was the Hindoo, the first necessities of whose life would be cheapened and not the Lancashire manufacturer, who would be benefited by the remission of the duty.[30] This explanation did not absolve Lord Salisbury from the attacks of Viscount Halifax and some other members of the House, who, on several other occasions, brought up the matter for comment and criticism.[31]

[28] Gt. Brit. Parliamentary Debates, 1889, 333 : 234—5. Quoted by Lord Stanley in his speech in the House of Lords.

[29] Gt. Brit. Parliamentary Debates, 1876, 227 : 1951—60.

[30] Ibid., pp. 1960—1975.

[31] Ibid., pp. 1976—2007.

After this time the question of the abolition of the import duty was again and again taken up in both Houses of Parliament. At last, on July 10, 1877, Mr. H. Birley, Manchester, moved a resolution in the House of Commons, which being amended passed as follows: — "That, in the opinion of this House, the duties now levied upon cotton manufactures imported into India, being protective[32] in their nature, are contrary to sound commercial policy, and ought to be repealed without delay, so soon as the financial condition of the country will permit".[33]

The Bombay Factory Commission of 1875.[34]

During the time when the tariff controversy was going on between the Secretary of State for India and the Governor General, the Governor of Bombay, on the advice of the former, appointed, on March 23, 1875, a commission for the investigation of factory conditions, with Mr. F. F. Arbuthnot, Collector of Bombay, as chairman. The commission was composed of eight members, some of whom represented the interests of the cotton industry. The principal subjects to which the commission paid special attention were as follows: (1) danger from machinery and the necessity of protection; (2) age of employment of children; (3) hours of work; (4) holidays; (5) sanitation; (6) ventilation; (7) education; (8) the necessity of legislation. The commission held 10 meetings, took the evidence of 26 witnesses including employers, employees, and physicians, and made their report on July 2nd of the same year.[35]

The condition of factory labor in the city of Bombay as revealed by the investigation and the recommendations

[32] It will be remembered that, on March 9, 1875, the Under Secretary of State for India objected, in the House of Commons, to the use of the words "protective" to the duties levied by the Government of India, which were really for revenue purposes only. Cf. *Supra*, p. 10.

[33] Gt. Brit. Parliamentary Debates, 1877, 235 : 1128.

[34] *Ibid.*, 1875, 224 : 158 and 1876, 227 : 301.

[35] *Ibid.*, 227 : 301, and the *Times*, London, Sept. 24, 1878, p. 3, c. 6. Report, Bombay Factory Commission of 1875, p. 2.

of the witnesses may be summarised as follows: — First, all the machinery was on the whole well protected, but some parts needed improvement. Second, the minimum age of the employment of children was 8 on an average, but some 6 and 7 year old children were also found working in the factory. The recommendation for minimum age varied from 7 to 14 years. Third, the hours of work generally extended from surise to sunset. The majority of witnesses recommended 10 hours for men and women, while, the general opinion on the working time for children varied from 4 to 10 hours. A few of the witnesses recommended fixing it to half the time of work for men. Fourth, on the average the factories worked from 300 to 320 days in the year. There was no fixed day for holiday. One holiday out of seven was the general recommendation. Fifth, the necessity of regulating ventilation in a factory was realized by all.[36]

The commission's report showed a division of opinion. The majority report consisted of the following conclusions: — First, inspite of apparently long hours of work, the physical condition of factory employees was good. This was probably due to the fact that they earned higher wages in the factories and were thus able to procure better and more substantial food than nine-tenths of the people of the same class employed as day laborers. Second, employees themselves would like to have their hours of work reduced, provided that their wages were not decreased at the same time.[37] Third, women and children, unlike their fellow workers in Lancashire, worked in a more or less natural atmosphere and, therefore, did not suffer any hardship, and lastly, that legislation for the regulation of factory labor was uncalled for.[38]

The minority report of two members, the President and Dr. Blainey, recommended, on the other hand, that the enactment of a simple law regulating the hours of work of children and requiring the proper fencing of machinery would be benefical both to employers and employees, and

---

[36] The Times, London, Nov. 14, 1890, p. 13, c. 2.
[37] Ibid., Sep. 24, 1878, p. 3, c. 6.
[38] Gt. Brit. Parliamentary Debates, 1877, 236 : 814.

that such an act should be passed by the Supreme Government and be applied to the whole of British India.[39]

Upon the receipt of the report, the Government of Bombay decided to make further inquiry outside the City of Bombay and directed the collectors of Broach and of Surat to gather evidence.[40] But sufficient evidence was not available to make out a case for factory legislation and Sir P. Wodehouse, Governor of Bombay, declined to take any further action in the matter on the ground that unnecessary interference would do more harm than good to the rising industry. Sir R. Temple, who soon succeeded Sir P. Wodehouse, concurred in the opinion of his predecessor, and for the time being, no further step was taken by the Government of Bombay.[41]

Agitation in India for Factory Legislation.

In the meantime, agitation, similar to that in England, was going on in India. While the public was apprehensive of the agitation of Manchester interests and of the official support they received at the India Office, looking upon it as an attempt to strangle the infant industry of India, the manufacturers were awakened to the necessity of protecting their interests. Philanthropists also were not lagging behind. Agitation was, therefore, started both by Indians and Europeans, for the regulation of labor in factories. Mr. Sorabjee Shapoorjee Bengalee played the leading role in this movement. Mr. Bengalee intended to bring the question of factory legislation before the Bombay Legislative Council and, with that object in view, drafted a bill with the following provisions:[42]

(1) No child should be employed in a factory before the age of eight.

(2) Daily hours of work for children between the ages of 8 and 14 should be limited to 9; for adult women over 14, to 10; and for adult men over 14, to 11;

---

[39] India, Legislative Council Proceedings, Calcutta, 1879, 18 : 240.

[40] Gt. Brit. Parliamentary Debates, 1876, 227 : 301.

[41] The Times, London, Sep. 24, 1878, p. 3, c. 6.

[42] Ibid., Sept. 18, 1878, p. 9, c. 4.

from these hours of work there must be set off an allowance of one hour for rest and meals for all classes of operatives.

(3) No child should be allowed to work for more than six days a week.[43]

(4) A register should be kept of the name, sex, and age of each person employed in each factory, the age to be certified by a surgeon appointed for the purpose by the Governor in Council.

(5) The chief police officer of the town or district should be charged with the duty of seeing that the provisions of the measure were duly obeyed.

After drafting the bill, Mr. Bengalee asked permission of the Bombay Government to introduce it into the Legislative Council. But he was informed by the Under-Secretary to the Government that such a bill could not be introduced into the local council and that the Bombay Government was unable even to report it to the Government of India, as the majority report did not show the existence of a case for even such limited legislation as proposed.[44]

Upon the rejection of his proposal by the Bombay Government, Mr. Bengalee appealed to Manchester for support. He sent 100 copies of his draft bill to Mr. John Croft of Manchester and requested him to distribute them among such people in England as were likely to take an interest in the matter. "I have, therefore", added Mr. Bengalee in a letter to Mr. Croft, and referring to the above rebuff, "no remedy left but to try what can be done through the English influence which, as a matter of course, is so potent with our governing classes".[45]

Revival of Agitation in England.

The refusal of the Bombay Government to take any action towards factory legislation revived the agitation of Manchester interests and their sympathisers. The publication

[43] Gt. Brit. Parliamentary Debates, 1879, 245 : 362.

[44] The Times, London, Sep. 18, 1878, p. 11, c. 2.

[45] Ibid., Sep. 13, 1878, p. 10, c. 1.

of Mr. Bengalee's appeal to Manchester in the Times of September 13, 1878,[46] was followed by several criticisms, rejoinders, and appeals. "Every member of that commission was more or less financially interested in Indian mills," humanity was "grossly outraged by the mill system of Bombay",[47] each mill in India was "a garrison", the laborers in an Indian factory looked like "a wretched crowd",[48] were some of the expressions used by the agitators. This subject was committed by others to the Times with the hope of eliciting its powerful aid "to do away with the iniquity", and "to press the matter upon the Government of India".[49] The condition of the new mills in India was considered by still others as a "scandal" to English civilization and a "reproach to the English name". On the other hand, defence of the conduct of the Bombay Government was not lacking even in England. Mr. A. Rogers, a former member of the Bombay Council, stated that as the children worked in pairs, the one off and the other on, the actual work did not amount to more than half of the nominal length of time. "Factory work is to them". concluded Mr. Rogers, "in fact, a well paid enjoyment".[50]

The Times, in commenting on the drastic character of Mr. Bengalee's bill, pointed out that embroidery work had exacted from the Indian woman long hours of listless toil for the poorest pay, while by working in a factory, she had her labor better paid and her existence penetrated by new light.[51] To the Hindu child, a meal earned by factory work was to be substituted for basking in the sun. Its life was monotonous and dull without the friction of new ideas and without mental development. Nursing and feeding a machine was a more liberal education than a Hindu child had received for thousands of years. While pointing out the importance of factory legislation, the

[46] The Times. London, Sept. 13, 1878, p. 10, c. 1.
[47] Ibid., Sept. 28, 1878, p. 11, c. 4.
[48] Ibid., Sept. 18, 1878, p. 11, c. 2.
[49] Ibid., Oct. 1, 1878, p. 8, c. 6.
[50] Gt. Brit. Parliamentary Debates, 1879, 245 : 353.
[51] The Times. London, Sept. 18, 1878. p. 9, c. 4.

editor remarked that it would be as unjust to Hindu women and children as to Bombay manufacturers to legislate in such a way as to banish female and child labor from the mills.[52]

At last, Lord Shaftsbury again appeared on the field, and in a letter to the Times, on October 2, 1878, offered his services, even at his extreme old age, to the cause of Indian factory laborers. "The remedy of the evil", continued the noble lord, "is a matter both of humanity and of justice, of humanity to the oppressed women and children and of justice to the mill owners of Lancashire, who are laid under restrictions from which the Indian mill owners are entirely free".[53]

On April 4, 1879, Lord Shaftsbury reopened the discussion on Indian factory legislation in the House of Lords. Describing at length, as before, the rapid growth of Indian factories and commenting on the report of the factory commission, Lord Shaftsbury tried to show the existence of abuses in Indian factories by quoting several expressions and passages of sensational character from different sources, some of which have been quoted above, and with an earnest appeal to their lordships to redress the misery of the "wretched" women in Indian mills, moved "That an humble address be presented to Her Majesty, praying that Her Majesty will be graciously pleased to instruct the Viceroy of India to take into immediate consideration the necessity of passing a law for regulating the labor of women and children in the mills and factories throughout Her dominions in India".[54]

In reply, Viscount Cranbrook, who had succeeded Lord Salisbury as Secretary of State for India, said that the subject of factory legislation had never been lost sight of by the Government of India. The delay in that direction had been due to two main causes: — First, the report of the commission, appointed for the purpose, was not favorable to any legislative measures; and second, the time for legislation was not opportune; owing to the prevalence of

[52] The Times, London, Sept. 18, 1878, p. 9, c. 3—5.
[53] Ibid., Oct. 3, 1878, p. 6, c. 4.
[54] Gt. Brit. Parliamentary Debates, 1879, 245 : 358.

famine during the years just preceding, the people were in distress and needed all the employment they could get. But the necessity of immediate legislation had already been realized by the Indian Government and a bill had also been prepared. Giving the assurance that he would do his utmost to impress upon the Government of India the urgency of legislation for the protection of women and children in factories, Lord Cranbrook requested their lordships not to address the Crown on this subject. The motion was, therefore, withdrawn by the leave of the House.[55]

In the meantime, several attempts had been made to reduce the import duty on cotton goods. Lord Northbrook had resigned and Lord Lytton had succeeded him as Governor General of India. As early as May 31, 1876, the Secretary of State in Council sent a dispatch to the Government of India in the following terms: — "The interests of India imperatively demand the timely removal of a tax which is at once wrong in principle, injurious in its practical effect, and self-destructive in its operation".[56] Afterwards several dispatches were exchanged on the subject between the Home Office in England and the Government of India. Early in 1879 Lord Lytton received a confidential dispatch from the Secretary of State and immediately after he reduced the duty, though the opinion of his council was strongly opposed to such a course.

The reduction of the duty by the action of the Governor General in overruling his Council, especially at a time when high expenditure was to be met by the Government due to the Afghan War, was strongly resented by the people of India. Fresh attacks were also made in the House of Commons on the conduct of Lord Lytton.[57] But the party representing Manchester interests was extremely strong in Parliament and, on April 4, 1879, Mr. W. E. Briggs, Blackburn, succeeded in passing another resolution

[55] Gt. Brit. Parliamentary Debates, 1879, 245 : 358—63.

[56] Ibid., p. 984.

[57] Ibid., pp. 983—84.

deprecating the import duty and asking for its complete removal.[58]

Introduction of the Bill into the Legislature.

In addition to the question of the import duty that of factory legislation had also been under consideration by the Government of India, as the Secretary of State assured the House of Lords. Even as early as April of 1877, and long before Mr. Bengalee's appeal reached England, the Government of India had come to the conclusion that legislation for some sort of restriction on labor in factories was necessary.[59] But the publication of Mr. Bengalee's letter probably had some effect in consequence of which his bill received more favorable consideration. The Government of Bombay approved of its provisions, and even the Government of India used it as a groundwork for the preparation of a new bill.[60] As it was decided by the Government of India that one act should be passed for the whole of India, the draft of the bill was first submitted to the different local governments. Early in 1879, the Governor of Bombay and the Lieutenant-Governor of Bengal expressed their concurrence in the principle of the bill.[61] The views of the other local governments having gradually been collected, the motion for leave to introduce the bill into the Legislative Council of India was at last made on October 17, 1879.

In making the motion Mr. B. W. Colvin stated that the inquiry sent to all local governments in order to ascertain the condition of labor in factories located in their districts, showed that the factory workers were, as a body, practically as well off as most persons of their class, who were not employed in factories, and in many respects they were better off. But the employment of children and the use of machinery furnished occasion for abuses, which had already appeared, and which were likely to increase with

[58] Gt. Brit. Parliamentary Debates, 1879, 245 : 375.

[59] Ibid., 1877, 236 : 815.

[60] Ibid., 1879, 245 : 362.

[61] Ibid., p. 363.

increasing competition not only in Bombay but in other provinces as well. A good case had thus been shown to exist for the enactment of a legislative measure regulating labor in the factories of the whole country. The act would be of a permissive but uniform character, applicable largely at the option of the local governments. The scope of the act would include two main objects: — First, the protection of children and of young persons who had not attained the age when they could protect themselves; and second, security to all employees from dangerous machinery. For the realization of these objects, a system of factory inspection would be introduced by the local governments and reports on accidents would be required from managers of factories, whenever they occurred.

Mr. Colvin urged that in the enactment of such an act three important things should always be kept in view: — First, there should be no interference with the freedom of employers and employees; they should be left at liberty to make any arrangements which they thought most conducive to their own interests. Second, the climatic and social differences between England and India were so great that the English law would not only be inapplicable but might be actually injurious to India. Third, nothing should be done which would check the growth of the manufacturing industry in India. From every point of view it was highly desirable that such industries should be given the utmost range of development in order to relieve the pressure of the agricultural population upon the land. Agriculture being practically the sole occupation of the people, the earning of a livelihood was becoming harder every day with the growth of population. The danger of such overcrowding became evident during the famine that had lately afflicted such large parts of the country.

Consideration by the Select Committee.

The bill was introduced into the legislature on November 7, 1879, its text consisting of the following principal points: —[62]

[62] British Medical Journal, Jan. 3, 1880, p. 28.

(1) Determination of the age at which children might be employed.
(2) Limitation of the hours of labor for children and young persons.
(3) Prohibition of the employment of children and young persons in certain dangerous work.
(4) Fencing of dangerous machinery.
(5) Reporting of accidents.
(6) Appointment of Government inspectors.

On the same day the bill was referred to a select committee.

The permissive character of the bill, however, gave rise to some sectional disputes in the country. The causes for factory legislation first appeared in Bombay, where a large number of women and children were employed. A permissive law would naturally have been applied to Bombay, whether other provinces adopted it or not. The people of Bombay, therefore, protested against this provision. The Sarvajanik Shabha, or the people's association, at Poona, raised objection on the ground that the measure, if sound in principle, should be made obligatory upon all provinces of India and that, if it was necessary to regulate labor in a particular province, the matter ought to be left to the local government concerned. But the worst feature of a permissive act, the Shabha contended, would be to put one province at a relative disadvantage as regards other provinces of the Empire.[63]

The bill was objected to for the further reason that the restrictions on the age would throw many children out of the factories and disorganize the whole factory work. In a memorial to the Under Secretary to the Government of Bombay, the Bombay Millowners' Association stated, on September 6, 1880, that the interests of the factories and of the children themselves would be best conserved by beginning the restriction at a comparatively low age which should be raised afterwards and that nothing would justify so high a maximum age limit for

[63] India, Legislative Council Proceedings, Calcutta, 1881, 20 : 100.

children as 14 years, which was contemplated in the bill. But even if 12 years were fixed as the ultimate proper limit for the maximum age, the association would suggest that it should at first be placed at 10 years, and raised in the future as necessity arose.[64]

These and similar objections were taken into consideration by the select committee in coming to conclusion. The bill as submitted by the select committee had the following notable provisions: —

(1) A factory was defined to mean any premises where work was carried on for not less than four months in the year, with the aid of steam, water or other mechanical power, and where not less than one hundred persons were employed at one time.[65]

(2) The minimum age of children in industry was fixed at 8 years and the maximum at 14, and their daily working hours at 9 instead of at 6, as originally proposed after the English law. The reasons for such a change in the working hours were: — First, the factory work in India was neither so severe nor so continuous as that in England. Second, an English child worked in a factory for six hours and attended school for three hours, which meant nine hours' work altogether; but the Indian child, as a rule, did not have to go to school. Third, the limitation of work to six hours might lead a child to work six hours in one factory and six hours more in another. Nine hours were not too long provided one hour's interval was given during the time for food and rest.

The hours of work for children being raised to nine, there was no necessity of creating a young person class with working hours of eight as originally proposed.

(3) The time at which the intervals of rest from labor should be given as well as the length of each interval itself, should be fixed by the local government for each factory after ascertaining, as far as possible, the existing

---

[64] Gt. Brit. Parl. Papers, 1888, Vol. 77, H. of C. 321, p. 9.

[65] India, Legislative Council Proceedings, Calcutta, 1881, 20 : 88. — The Crown factories were also to be brought under the Act, as in Great Britain. The power to exempt them temporarily in case of need was, however, to be reserved by the Government.

practice in such factory and the wishes of the manager thereof.

(4) The bill gave the local governments power to require a register to be kept of children employed in a factory.

There was no provision regarding sanitation, though the Governments of Bombay and Madras gave their opinion that such provision was needed. The committee thought that no necessity for such a provision had been shown to exist. Some municipal acts, like that of Bombay, allowed the government sufficient power in these matters. Moreover, the subject might be taken up by the local government, if necessary.

One of the principal recommendations of the select committee was that the act should be made compulsory for the whole of India. Otherwise, it would put the factories of one province at a comparative disadvantage over those of others, thus creating ill-feeling among the provinces.

Passage of the Bill.

On March 11, 1881, the report of the select committee was taken into consideration by the Legislative Council. The main point at issue in the discussion was the compulsory character of the proposed act. The necessity of such a measure for regulating labor in factories was first questioned by Maharaja Jotindra Mohan Tagore. He maintained that the authoritative intervention between labor and capital in a country where the manufacturing industry was still in its infancy was quite undesirable. European capital and energy were gradually being drawn into the country. Any uncalled for legislative interference resulting in the check of industrial development would be a great misfortune to the country. But he directed his main attack against the decision of the select committee of which he himself was a member, for a compulsory and uniform law applicable to all British India. He pointed out that there was a difference of opinion as to the necessity of such a measure even in Bombay where the abuses were alleged to exist. India was a vast country and the conditions in different parts were so different that what might be good for one part might not be good for another part. If the peculiar condition of one province called for some particular law, it was unjust to extend that law to another province where there was no need for it. In Bengal, compulsory labor legislation not only was unnecesary; but would be positively injurious. Owing to the absence of any great competition and to their unity of interest, the capitalist and the laborer in that section of India worked in harmony. Forced legislation of the kind contemplated might, on the contrary, create friction and discord by tempting both classes to stand too rigidly on their respective legal rights and thus perhaps strangle a young industry, which had opened the means of livelihood to thousands of the poorer classes.

Mr. Kennedy also opposed the compulsory character of the bill and said that the evils, real or supposed, had sprung up in the treatment of the children who were employed in the cotton factories of Bombay. The factory owners in Bengal had not given any occasion for these restrictive measures. Industries other than the cotton manufacture conducted in this country were not likely to interfere with the interests of any great and powerful body of English manufacturers, who undoubtedly looked upon the cotton manufacture of India with a by no means friendly eye. He, therefore, made a motion to exempt Bengal from the operation of the proposed act.

Mr. H. J. Reynolds, in defending the conclusions of the select committee, of which he was a member, pointed out that if the act were permissive, its application to one province and not to another would cause strong resentment. He also added that there was another argument, which had seemed to him to point in the same direction. "There is", he said, "a very general opinion, at any rate outside the Council Chamber, that this legislation has been urged upon the Government of India from two very different and opposite quarters — the voice is the voice of Exeter Hall, but the hand is the hand of Manchester. If there is any foundation for this belief, it will follow that the instigators of the measure will not be satisfied with the mere passing of a permissive bill; but will put pressure on the Government to enforce the Act in every part of the country in which a mill or a factory can be found".[66]

Before the discussion proceeded further, the Government proposed to amend the bill as reported by the select committee. The main object of the amendment was to change the restrictive character of the bill in order to meet the reasonable wishes of those who objected to the stringency of the measure, and at the same time to maintain the contention of the Government that some kind of legislation was necessary to protect those who could not protect themselves. The amendment brought about two principal changes: First, the minimum and maximum age limits of children were reduced from 8 and 14 to 7 and 12 respectively in order to remove some difficulties in giving effect to the law.[67] It had been represented to the Government that the age of 7 was more in consonance with the practice of the employment in India. Second, the obligatory character of the provision dealing with the appointment of special inspectors was also changed and it was left to the discretion of the local governments either to appoint a special inspector or to invest the magistrate of the district with necessary power for supervision. The Bengal Government contended that it would be hard to find a properly qualified person for such a position and that the Bengal employers were opposed to such an idea. On the other hand, added the Bengal Government, the casual inspection of a factory by the highest official of a district could scarcely be objected to by any person.

After other changes of minor importance, such as the exclusion of tea and coffee plantations and indigo works from the operation of the proposed act were made in the bill, it was passed on April 15, 1881, and the new act was called the "Indian Factories Act, 1881", being Act No. XV of 1881 and came into force on July 1, 1881.

---

[66] India, Legislative Council Proceedings, Calcutta, 1881, 20 : 144. The Governor General informed the Council that the above opinion was unfounded.

[67] India, Legislative Council Proceedings, Calcutta, 1881, 20 : 95—96.

Chief Provisions of the Act.

1. It was to apply to all manufacturing premises using power driven machinery, employing 100 or more persons and working more than four months in the year, indigo, tea and coffee plantations being exempted from the provisions of the Act.

2. The age limits for the employment of children were fixed at 7 and 12 years. Their hours of work were limited to 9 in any one day with an interval of rest for one hour. They were also granted four monthly holidays.

3. Engine flyheads and hoists, and other dangerous machinery at the option of the inspector had to be fenced.

4. Accidents had to be reported to the inspector.

5. The local governments could appoint special inspectors, otherwise district magistrates would become inspectors in their respective jurisdictions.

6. The local governments also had power to make rules for carrying out the provisions of the Act.

CHAPTER III.

FACTORY ACT OF 1891.

Agitation in England for Amendment.

The most significant feature of the Factory Act of 1881 was the establishment of the fact that the Government would interfere with the industrial relations of the people, whenever a class or a party, was unable to protect its own interests. This resulted in the regulation of child labor in Indian factories. The measure was, of course, inadequate to meet all phases of the problem, but a beginning was made and a principle was established for the subsequent development of the regulative function of the Government regarding factory labor. But the establishment of a theoretical principle could neither satisfy the matter-of-fact commercial interests of Lancashire, whose spirit of rivalry was goaded by the rising manufacturing industry in India, nor pacify the idealistic mind of the philanthropists, who had been striving to redress the actual misery of the working people in Indian factories. The agitation, therefore, continued both in England and in India as before, though in varying degrees.

In the very year the act was passed, Lancashire manufacturers sustained a still further loss of their trade with India. The import of cotton twist and yarn into India declined from 45,877,000 lbs. in 1880—1881 to 40,762,000 lbs. in 1881—1882, and of cotton piece goods, from 1,776,507 yds. to 1,624,452 yds.[1]

The former market for cotton twist and yarn was not regained until the year 1885—1886. But even then the trade for cotton piece goods was far below that of 1880—1881.[2] During the same period of five years from 1880—1881 to 1885—1886, the number of cotton factories in India increased from 62 to 89 with a corresponding increase in the number of spindles from 1,550,944 to 2,198,545 and, of looms from 14,386 to 16,548. On the

[1] Gt. Brit. Parl. Papers, 1894, Vol. 59, H. of C. 43, p. 311.
[2] Ibid.
[3] Ibid.

other hand, the Indian export trade greatly extended during the period. The export of cotton twist and yarn increased from 26,901,000 lbs. to 78,242,000 lbs. and of cotton piece goods from 30,385,000 yds. to 51,528,000 yds. as shown on the table below: —

Growth of the Cotton Industry
from 1880—1881 to 1885—1886.

	1880—1881	1885—1886
Factories	62	89
Looms	14,386	16,548
Spindles	1,550,944	2,198,545
Twist and Yarn exports	26,901,000 lbs.	78,242,000 lbs.
Piece goods exports	30,385,000 yds.	51,528,000 yds.

In short, at the end of five years, when England was just regaining her export trade in cotton goods into India, India herself was increasing her export trade into foreign markets by 190.9 per cent in cotton twist and yarn and by 69 per cent in cotton piece goods.[4] Under these circumstances it was not probable that Manchester interests would feel at rest until the import duty on their goods was totally abolished.

On November 10, 1881, the Manchester Chamber of Commerce sent a deputation to the India Office for an interview with Lord Hartington, who was then the Secretary of State for India, again to urge the repeal of the import duty on cotton goods by the Indian Government. Lord Hartington assured the Chamber that the question had never been lost sight of and that both the Indian Government and the Home Government were fully alive to the fulfillment of the promise given before.[5] The promise was soon carried out. In 1882, the Indian Government completely repealed the import duty.[6] The Manchester interests thus won the first object of their agitation.

[4] Gt. Brit. Parl. Papers, 1894, Vol. 59, H. of C. 43, p. 311.
[5] The Times, London, Nov. 12, 1881, p. 11, c. 1.
[6] Gt. Brit. Parl Papers, 1903, Vol. 46, H. of C. 249, p. 190.

Agitation in India for Amendment.

It has already been observed that the provision of the Factory Act of 1881 was too inadequate to meet the demand of the philanthropic agitators. Even the Governor General is said to have expressed a doubt as to the wisdom of reducing the minimum age of children from eight to seven and, in the circular issued to the local governments regarding the administration of the new act a few days before it came into force, directed the local authorities to watch this provision very closely.[7] No sooner was the act passed than agitation was started afresh in Bombay for its amendment. Both Europeans and Indians soon joined the cause under the championship of Mr. Bengalee.[8]

Sir James Ferguson, who was then the Governor of Bombay and who had been personally advised by the Secretary of State for India to carry through the Indian factory legislation before he left for India, warmly supported the agitation,[9] and made an application for the temporary services of one of the British factory inspectors in order to supervise and report on the working of the factory act in Bombay. Mr. Redgrave, chief inspector of factories in Great Britain, who a few years before had suggested the enactment of legislation for Indian factories, recommended Mr. Meade King, an inspector of cotton factories in the district of Manchester, for the work.[10] Mr. King arrived at Bombay early in 1882, and, after about six months' investigation made his report on July 7, 1882.[11] He found many inadequacies in the existing law and made several recommendations, of which the following were the chief:[12]

(1) That no child under 8 should be employed in a factory and that 13 was quite old enough for an Indian child to commence full-time work.

---

[7] The Times, London, June 13, 1881, p. 7, c. 1.
[8] Gt. Brit. Parl. Papers, 1888, Vol. 26, C. 5328, p. 113.
[9] Ibid.
[10] Ibid., 1883, Vol. 18, C. 3488, p. 11.
[11] Ibid., 1888, Vol. 77, H. of C. 321, p. 13.
[12] Ibid., pp. 6—11.

(2) That all children should be examined by certifying surgeons regarding their age and physical fitness previous to employment in factories.

(3) That a young person class above 13 and below 16 should be created.

(4) That women and children should be allowed to work only between 6 A. M. and 6 P. M., and that during that period they should have an hour's period for food and rest, either a full one hour in the middle of the day, or two half-hours with a convenient spell of work between them.

(5) That cleanliness and ventilation should be secured in all factories.

Bombay Factory Commission of 1884.

With a view to ascertaining the advisability of extending Mr. King's suggestions to textile and other factories, and to considering the subject in all its bearings,[13] the Government of Bombay appointed a commission on May 23, 1884; and, in order to facilitate the work of the commission, a medical commitee was also appointed on September 3, 1884. The medical committee was advised to inquire into the general health and physical condition of mill workers as compared with that of other laborers in the city of Bombay and to place the results of their investigation before the commission. On October 16, 1884, the sanitary commissioner of Bombay was also authorized to examine into the sanitary condition of factories and workshops in that presidency and to give evidence before the commission.[14]

The commission which was organized soon after its appointment consisted of eight members, including Mr. W. B. Mulock, collector of Bombay, as president with a casting vote. The Bombay Chamber of Commerce and Mill-Owners' Association each had two representatives. Mr. Bengalee, chief advocate for factory legislation, and

[13] Gt. Brit. Parl. Papers, 1888, Vol. 77, H. of C. 321, p. 3.

[14] Ibid.

Dr. Thos. Blainey, a member of the factory commission of 1875, who voted in favour of factory legislation, were also nominated as members of this commission.[15]

The medical committee[16] was organized when the commission was sitting. The members of the committee closely examined 265 male laborers, after carefully ascertaining their height and weight,[17] but found no evidence of the alleged deterioration in the health of factory operatives as compared with that of other laborers in the city of Bombay. They suggested, however, some changes in the existing law as a precautionary measure, and advised fixing the minimum age of children for employment in factories at 10 years and granting four holidays in a month to all operatives, irrespective of age or sex.[18] The sanitary commissioner, in his exhaustive report, also stated that the condition of factories was generally far from being as bad as he had been led to expect. He was nevertheless of the opinion that they needed some better arrangement regarding ventilation, latrine accomodation, etc.[19]

But the most significant thing in connection with the commission was the calling of a labor conference by the Bombay factory operatives. The prime mover of this conference was, of course, Mr. Bengalee but it was organized by Mr. N. M. Lokhanday. The main object of the conference was to present the grievances of factory workers to the commission. The conference held its meetings on September 23 and 26, 1884, and drew up a memorial to the commission,

---

[15] Gt. Brit. Parl. Papers, 1888, Vol. 77, H. of C. 321, p. 3. Messrs. G. Cotton and J. L. Symons represented the Bombay Chamber of Commerce and Messrs. Nanabhoy B. Jeejibhoy and Muncherjee Nowrajee Banajee, the Bombay Mill-Owners' Association. The other member was Khan Bahadur Muncherjee C. Murzaban.

[16] The committee consisted of Surgeons Majors I. B. Lyon, W. Gray, and G. Waters, and also of Mr. N. H. Chokshi, L. M. S. Gt. Brit. Parl. Papers, 1888, Vol. 77, H. of C. 321, p. 3.

[17] Ibid., 1907, Vol. 59, Cd. 3617, p. 19.

[18] Ibid., 1888, Vol. 77, H. of C. 321, p. 12.

[19] Ibid., p. 6.

which was signed by 5,500 employees and contained the following resolutions:[20]

(1) That all mill-hands be allowed one complete day of rest every Sunday.

(2) That half an hour's recess be allowed them at noon every working day.

(3) That work in mills should commence at 6.30 A. M. and close at sunset.

(4) That payment of wages should be made not later than the 15th of the month following that for which they have been earned.

(5) That a workman sustaining serious injury in the course of his work at the mill, which might disable him for the time being, should receive full wages until he recovers, and that in case of his being maimed for life, suitable provision should be made for his livelihood.

In the meantime the members of the commission also finished their investigation. They had held 27 meetings, examined 34 witnesses, including employers, employees, and factory inspectors, and had personally inspected several mills and workshops. They had duly considered the reports of the medical committee and of the sanitary commissioner as well as the memorial of factory operatives, and, after fully discussing Mr. Meade King's suggestions, they forwarded the results of their investigations to the Government of Bombay on January 10, 1885.[21] The principal recommendations of the commission were: —

(1) To raise the minimum age of the children from 7 to 9 and the maximum from 12 to 14, except in the case of children with some educational attainments, under which circumstances the age limits might be 8 and 13 respectively. These changes were necessary for several reasons: — First, the higher temperature in Indian mills and the weaker physical development of the people as well as the small practical value of the labor of children were sufficient reasons why the minimum age should be raised to nine.

[20] Gt. Brit. Parl. Papers, 1890—91, Vol. 59, H. of C. 86, p. 106.
[21] Ibid., 1888, Vol. 77, H. of C. 321, p. 18.

Second, the medical committee recommended raising it to 10. But the commission thought that such a change would be too sudden and would throw many children out of employment. All changes should be made gradually, as in the case of the English factory law. Third, the Bombay Millowners' Association in their memorial to the Government of Bombay in 1880 foresaw,[22] and calculated on, such an increase of age for children. Fourth, an earlier admission into the first employment and an earlier transition into adult employment, permitted on the condition of educational attainments, would result in furthering the interests of both employers and employees since Indian operatives would be trained in a way similar to that which proved successful in England.

(2) To require all children to be certified of age and physical fitness before employment, as suggested by Mr. Meade King.[23]

(3) To limit the time of the day, during which a child could work, to the period between 7 A. M. and 5 P. M. with an hour's interval for meal and rest. Until school accommodation could be supplied and general arrangements could be made for educating working children and obliging them to attend school for a portion of the working day, or on alternate days, the only way to force the statutory limitation of nine for a child's labor was to fix a period of employment, as suggesed above.[24]

(4) To raise gradually the age limits of children, thereby avoiding the necessity of creating a young person class under sixteen, as suggested by Mr. King. Sufficient difficulty had already been experienced in determining the ages of children. The creation of a young person class would complicate still more the situation in a country, where there was no system of birth registration.[25]

(5) To incorporate several provisions of the British factory act into the Indian factory law and to improve the sanitary condition of factories, e. g., ventilation, lime-

---

22 Gt. Brit. Parl. Papers, 1888, Vol. 77, H. of C. 321, p. 9.
23 Ibid., p. 11.
24 Ibid., pp. 7—10.
25 Ibid., p. 10.

washing, etc. The commission observed that the condition of the factory exercised a marked influence on the character of its operatives. Furthermore, it recommended that standard plans for the construction of mills should be carefully prepared so that future mills could be built according to such plans.[26]

(6) To grant four monthly holidays to women and children. The existing law granted such holidays only to children. The commission recommended the extension of this provision to women. These holidays should be on Sundays, whenever possible. On the occurrence of an important native holiday during the week, preference should be given to it for rest, work being done on the following or preceding Sunday.[27]

Mr. Bengalee and Dr. Blainey differed from the majority of the commission on this point. They recommended that all operatives, male or female, should be entitled to one day of rest each week in addition to their 15 native holidays. They based their recommendations on the following grounds: — First, there was a consensus of opinion among the witnesses regarding such statutory holidays for all operatives. Second, the working people themselves prayed for this reasonable boon in their memorial to the Government of Bombay. Third, the prohibition of work for women and children on Sundays would not secure these holidays to adult male operatives in India. Those who relied on such a result had, of course, in mind the system in England. But the conditions in the two countries were different. Women and children formed only 25 per cent of the total operatives in India as against the 74 per cent of the same classes of operatives in England. Moreover, women worked only in reeling and winding departments, which could be easily separated from the main part of the factory.[28] Fourth, the *laissez-faire* doctrine, under the influence of which the majority of the commission declined to recommend legislation on behalf of adult males, was not observed even in Great Britain as

[26] Gt. Brit. Parl. Papers, 1888, Vol. 77, H. of C. 321, pp. 5—6.
[27] *Ibid.*, pp. 10—11.
[28] *Ibid.*, p. 18.

far as legislation in the cause of humanity and morals was concerned.[29]

(7) To extend the scope of the Act to factories employing 10 or more women and children and using mechanical power. The commission had collected a large amount of evidence which proved that gross abuses existed in seasonal employments, especially in cotton gins and presses in the district of Khandesh, Bombay. These establishments employed mostly women and children, who worked in insanitary and ill-ventilated buildings from 4 or 5 in the morning till 8 or 9 in the evening. Sometimes the gins worked day and night for seven or eight days together. The commission recommended that women and children in such establishments should be allowed to work for 16 hours with two hours' interval for rest and food. Any strict legislation, it was thought, would "deprive these wretched women of their employment"[30] or lower the small pittance they already received.

The other recommendations were of minor importance.

The Government of Bombay acted very favorably on the report of the commission. But it failed to perceive the advisabilty of permitting children to be employed one year earlier on an educational test, its objection to such employment of children being based on physical, and not educational, grounds.[31] The Government of Bombay, however, forwarded the report to the Government of India with the hope that the Governor General in Council might see fit to amend the existing law, as proposed by the commission;[32] but the Government of India declined to take any action in the direction of general legislation.[33]

Revival of Agitation in England.

Shortly after, Mr. Jones, former inspector of British factories, who had been appointed, in September of 1883, by the Government of Bombay to take the place of Mr.

---

[29] Gt. Brit. Parl. Papers, 1888, Vol. 77, H. of C. 321, p. 18.
[30] Ibid., p. 15.
[31] Ibid., p. 20.
[32] Ibid., p. 22.
[33] Ibid., 1889, Vol. 58, H. of C. 124, p. 63.

Meade King, and who had served as secretary to the factory commission,[34] resigned his post and arrived in England, in May 1887, where he was reappointed as inspector of factories in the district of Manchester, Blackburn, Oldham, etc., with his headquarters at Manchester.[35]

After the resumption of his duties, Mr. Jones, at the request of Mr. Redgrave, chief inspector of British factories, who has been referred to twice before, made a statement on the condition of Indian factories, which appeared in the report on British factories and workshops,[36] and which criticised the Indian factory system on four main points: — (1) Long hours of work and few holidays. (2) Occasional withholdings of wages from employees. (3) Incompetency of mill managers and dangerous character of many mills. (4) Ill-ventilated and filthy state of many work rooms.[37] "The question of factory legislation", concluded Mr. Jones, referring to the decision of the Government of India on the report of the factory commission, "has been shelved, and sometime must elapse before another effort will be made, unless pressure be brought to bear upon the Home Government".[38]

Some of Mr. Jones' allegations were not based on facts, as will be shown later, but they did not fail to produce their effect. On May 3, 1888, not long after the publication of Mr. Jones' statement, Lord Cross, then Secretary of State for India, directed the Government of India to report on the following points: — (1) Working of the Factory Act; (2) working of the system of inspection by district magistrates; (3) accidents in factories; and (4) the defects pointed out by Mr. Jones. Agitation was also immediately started in Parliament. Messrs. Samuel Smith and James MacLean, the latter member representing

[34] Gt. Brit. Parl. Papers, 1888, Vol. 77, H. of C. 321, pp. 22—23. It was proposed to the Government of India to grant Mr. Jones an honorarium of 500 rupees in consideration of the services rendered by him as secretary to the commission, but the Government of India declined to sanction the grant.

[35] Ibid., 1888, Vol. 26, C. 5328, p. 10.

[36] Ibid.

[37] Ibid., 1889, Vol. 58, H. of C. 162, p. 2.

[38] Ibid., 1888, Vol. 26, C. 5328, p. 114.

Oldham, drew the attention of the House of Commons to the absence of provision for regulating the hours of work and other shortcomings in Indian factories, and asked whether it was not advisable to apply the English factory law to India.[39] These interrogations resulted in a further dispatch, on July 26, 1888, by the Secretary of State who directed the Government of India to consider whether or not it was expedient to regulate by law the working hours of women and to grant a legal weekly holiday to all factory operatives.[40] The Government of India consequently issued orders, on June 21 and August 28, 1888, to all local governments to report on the inquiries made by the Secretary of State.[41]

Meanwhile India was making still further progress in her new industrial career. In the five years from 1885—86 to 1890—91, the number of cotton factories rose from 89 to 125, and the number of spindles increased from 2,198,545, to 3,197,740, and of looms from 16,548 to 23,846, as shown in the table below:

Growth of the Cotton Industrv
from 1885—86 to 1890—91.

	1885—86	1890—91
Factories	89	125
Looms	16,548	23,845
Spindles	2,198.545	3,197,740

During the same period, while her imports of twist and yarn rose from 45,915,000 to 50,971,000 lbs., and of coton piece goods from 1,743,378 to 2,014,443 yds., her exports of cotton twist and yarn rose from 78,242,000 lbs., to 169,275,000 lbs., and of cotton piece goods from 51,528,000 yards to 67,639,000 yards, as shown in the table below:[42]

[39] Gt. Brit. Parl. Papers, 1889, Vol. 58, H. of C. 162, p. 2.
[40] Ibid., p. 60.
[41] Ibid., H. of C. 124, p. 3.
[42] Ibid., 1894, Vol. 59, H. of C. 43, p. 311.

Comparative Growth of Imports and Exports in Cotton Goods from 1885—86 to 1890—91.

Cotton Goods	Imports		Exports	
	1885-86	1890—91	1885—86	1890—91
Twist and yarn . . (in pounds)	45,915,000	50,971,000	78,242,000	169,275,000
Piece Goods . . . (in yards)	1.743,378	2,014,443	51,528 000	67.639,000

The period between January 1888 and June 1889 was one of marked expansion of the cotton industry in the Presidency of Bombay. While the export of cotton yarn to China and Japan kept pace with the increase in production, the export of cotton piece goods in 1888 exceeded that in 1887 to the extent of 13,500,000 yards.[43]

This rapid growth of the cotton industry in the latter half of the eighties, especially that of the year 1888, again gave Manchester interests cause for considerable anxiety. To their amazement, they found that in the course of six years the export of Indian cotton yarn to China and Japan had increased by 300,000,000 lbs., whereas the export of English cotton yarn to those countries had decreased by about 30,000,000 lbs.[44] They had already secured a market in India free from any import duty and on equal terms with the local manufacturers, but they had not yet been able to enforce the English factory law on India and it was to this phase of their agitation that they now turned their attention.

A meeting of the Manchester Chamber of Commerce was held on November 5, 1888, and a resolution was carried by a vote of 38 to 28 to the effect that in view of the excessive hours of labor in the cotton mills of British India, the British factory acts so far as they related to

[43] Gt. Brit. Parl. Papers, 1890, Vol. 53, H. of C. 384, p. 179.
[44] The Times, London, March 23, 1889, p. 5, c. 4.

the employment of women, young persons, and children, should be extended to include the textile factories of India.[45] The resolution was proposed on the ground of humanity towards Indian operatives. But Mr. Stuttard, who seconded the resolution, disclosed the real motive in his letter to the Manchester Courier, "Surely it will be better for the physical welfare of the Hindoo to remain in agricultural employment and give us plenty of cotton, rather than be attracted to the ranks of mill operatives".[46]

On March 22, 1889, a deputation representing the Lancashire factory operatives waited on Lord Cross, the Secreetary of State for India, and Sir John Gorst, the Under Secretary, at the India Office, in reference to "the condition of their fellow work people in India".[47] The deputation was headed by Mr. J. M. MacLean, and accompanied by Mr. Sidebottom and three other members of Parliament. In introducing the deputation, Mr. MacLean made the following complaints: — (1) that the British work people rightly considered that they had a real grievance in having to compete with Indian mill operatives, who were employed for perhaps 80 or more hours a week, (2) that this matter could not safely be left to the Government of India, as that Government never acted on the report of the Factory Commission of 1884, until his lordship being moved by the report of the chief inspector of British factories, asked what the view taken by that Government on the question was; (3) that the object of the deputation was to convey to his lordship the attitude of a considerable body of public opinion of the country on the question and to let his lordship know the feeling of the working people of Lancashire; and (4) that if the Indian mills were to be allowed to work night and day, Sunday and weekday, it was obvious that the British working men must be placed under very great disadvantage in competition in the markets of the world. Mr. Sidebottom added that mills in India were being built on a colossal scale, while there was only one mill in course of construction in the whole

[45] Gt. Brit. Parliamentary Debates, 1889, 333 : 232.
[46] Ibid., p. 332. Quoted by Lord Stanley of Alderley.
[47] The Times, London, March 23, p. 5, c. 4.

cotton district of Lancashire, and that the export of Indian cotton yarn was rapidly increasing and that of the English yarn was decreasing. He also urged that these things should be borne in mind in considering the question. In reply, Lord Cross assured the deputation that the Indian factory law would be amended to remedy the defects complained of.[48]

Counter-agitation in India.

The resolution of the Manchester Chamber of Commerce and their agitation to enforce the British factory law on Indian factories awakened a strong feeling of apprehension and resentment in India. The subject was extensively discussed in the press and severe criticism was directed against Manchester interests.[49] Even the *Times of India*, an Anglo-Indian Journal at Bombay, devoted to the British interests in India, writing on the resolution of the Manchester Chamber of Commerce, on November 30, 1888, said: — "We have to thank this minority for so clearly exposing the motive behind this ingenious attempt to lift the people of India." But it was the manufacturers who felt their position most insecure. The success of the Manchester agitation regarding the Indian import duty brought home to them the belief that the Manchester party might again succeed in forcing the British factory law on India and thereby retard the growth of the industry in which they invested millions of their capital. They, therefore, made a strong protest against the new Manchester movement.

Mr. D. Rasbotham of the Madras Chamber of Commerce, in a letter to the Government of India, on December 5, 1888, protested against the assertion by Manchester of a claim to have Indian labor regulated by the labor rivalry elsewhere. "The proposed extension of the British factory regulations to India", continued Mr. Rasbotham, "is not prompted by disinterested concern for the well-being of Indian operatives. The success which rewarded

[48] The *Times*, London, March 23, 1889, p. 5, c. 4.
[49] Gt. Brit. Parl. Papers, 1890, Vol. 53, H. of C. 384, p. 179.

the previous agitation was well calculated to encourage further interference with legislation in this country, such as never be proposed with regard to Canada or Australia; and this chamber apprehends that the opposition offered in Manchester to such interference is more likely to diminish than increase unless the Government of India takes an early opportunity of assuring the Secretary of State, that the assertions about the length and severity of hours of labor in this country are greatly exaggerated. The alleged desire to lift up the poor people of India and to improve their condition has so little to do with the demand for justice for Indian operatives that it may be eliminated from the consideration of the subject; whereas 'dictates of jealousy', the wish 'not so much to benefit a class in India as to recover the China market', 'self-interest', the discovery that 'competition in India was too severe', 'the interest of Lancashire trade' and not 'the interests of humanity' to which allusion was made at the meeting under notice, may be reasonably supposed to have exerted some influence on the supporters of the motion".[50]

On December 19, 1888, the Bombay Millowners' Association also protested against the resolution of the Manchester Chamber of Commerce by a counter-resolution. They pointed out that they worked only during the daylight hours, which did not allow them more than 13 hours and 13 minutes in summer and 11 hours in winter. Sixty-five per cent of the operatives in Lancashire were women; and work such as they did was done by men in India. For the same amount of work three and one third as many operatives were employed in India as in Lancashire. Moreover, Indian operatives took a long vacation every year.[51]

Meanwhile, in reply to the orders issued by the Government of India, on June 21 and August 28, 1888, the local governments submitted their reports and expressed their opinion. The Government of Bombay advocated the restriction of hours of labor for women and children and the granting of four legal monthly holidays to them, as in

[50] Gt. Brit. Parl. Papers, 1889, Vol. 58, H. of C. 124, p. 29.
[51] Gt. Brit. Parliamentary Debates, 1889, 333 : 232—33.

their previous resolution. In reply to the charges made by Mr. Jones, the Government of Bombay, against which the attack was mainly directed, said that the gentleman himself showed that the grievances or defects which he deemed most noticeable were, in the main,[52] either imaginary, or had full compensatory advantages as a set-of; that the hours of work in Indian factories were rather long, but the work was neither as heavy nor as intensive as that in English factories; that payment of wages was often delayed, but they were never withheld from operatives; that sanitary conditions were not bad considering the climate of the country and the habits of the people; and that the mill managers were fully competent for their work.[53]

The reports of other local governments also corroborated the statement of the Bombay Government. "The mills in this Presidency", reported the Government of Madras, "are in the hands of competent managers and are in good sanitary condition; machinery is adequately fenced, and no absuses in the way of withholding wages from the hands are found to exist".[54] With the exception of the Bombay Government, all other local governments were opposed to further restriction on factories by legislation. "It appears to the chief commissioner", replied the Government of the Central Provinces, "that no case exists, so far as these provinces are concerned, for further legislation".[55] "All officers deprecate", added the Government of Burma, "the modification of the factory act of 1881 in the direction of additional severity".[56] The replies of the Punjab Government and of the divisional officers of Lahore, and other localities were practically the same.

The Government of India submitted these reports to the Secretary of State on March 5, 1889, and added that the application of the English factory act to India was not expedient, and that the system of inspection by district

[52] Gt. Brit. Parl. Papers, 1889, Vol. 58, H. of C. 124, pp. 63—64.
[53] Ibid.
[54] Ibid., p. 3.
[55] Ibid., p. 52.
[56] Ibid., p. 61.

magistrates was quite adequate and satisfactory. The Government conceded the extending of the scope of the Indian factory act to cover smaller factories, the raising of the age limits of children from 7 and 12 to 9 and 14 respectively, the reducing of the working hours of women to 11 hours a day, and the bringing about of some other minor changes, but refused, at the same time, to grant four holidays a month to women and children by legislation.[57] On May 14, 1889, the Secretary of State accepted in a telegraphic dispatch, the proposal of the Governor-General but advised him to provide four holidays in a month for women and children by statutory enactment and also to make some other minor changes.[58]

Labor's Demand for Legislation.

In the agitation, which was going on in India, the exact wants of the employees were often misrepresented by employers and it was also said that employees themselves were indifferent to "any direct measure of protection against their employers" or did not feel the necessity of it. In order to show the real nature of their grievances, the labourers employed in the spinning and weaving mills of Bombay, submitted a petition to the Governor General of India on October 24, 1889. The petition originated among philanthropists like Mr. Bengalee and Mr. Lokhanday who had been agitating for the amendment of the factory act, and contained the resolutions of the employees passed at the conference in 1884 with some additional observations. Regarding the Sunday holiday, the petition stated that:[59] —

(a) It would contribute to the health and energy of employees, which would result in better work, both as to quality and quantity, and would thus benefit employers as well.

(b) It would afford workmen the much needed opportunity of attending to their household duties, especially

---

[57] Gt. Brit. Parl. Papers, 1889, Vol. 58, H. of C. 124, pp. 2—5.

[58] Ibid., p. 5.

[59] Ibid., 1890—91, Vol. 59, H. of C. 86 pp. 106—107.

shopping, which for lack of time, they were obliged to do with hawkers at exhorbitant prices.

(c) The loss to the millowners from overtaxing the energy of their employees by the unnatural system of incessant work for nearly 13 or 14 hours a day, was far greater than they were aware of.

(d) In the whole of British India, Sunday was considered a privileged holiday. Factory workers who did not obtain leave on that day could not afford to meet their relatives and friends, who were otherwise employed on week days.

(e) Employees did not enjoy more than 11 holidays in the year on account of religious festivals, though it had been alleged in certain quarters that their work did not amount to more than 300 days in the year.

(f) Under the existing system, workers were compelled to absent themselves from factories to attend to household duties and, for doing so, they had to lose two days' wages for one day's absence. This statement could be easily verified by reference to the muster-rolls kept in mills. As to the half hour's recess at midday, the petition called attention to the fact that actually it did not amount to more than 15 or 20 minutes. Much of this scanty recess was again taken up by the system of delivering up tickets at the time, an inconvenience which could be avoided by the time-keeper going around among employees while they were at work, and checking the ticket number off the musterroll.

With regard to the commencement of work in the morning, the petition said that uncertainty then prevailing with regard to the hour for starting work was very embarrassing and was the source of great inconvenience and discomfort to employees. A fixed and uniform hour of attendance was, therefore, greatly needed.

As to the payment of wages, the petition pointed out that the great delay in payment caused a good deal of inconvenience to the employees, and added that if the millowners desired a sort of hold on their employees to prevent desertion, the necessity of the case would be fully met by retaining in their hands a fortnight's wages of the men in arrears. In this connection, the petition also stated that cases in which employers illegally withheld the hard-earned wages of the poor workers were so frequent that a reference to the court of small causes would convince the government that wages were in many cases recovered only by recourse to the court. Hundreds of operatives had to forego their wages on account of the trouble involved in appealing to the judges. Most of the strikes in the factories would on inquiry be found to be attributable to the witholdings of wages in this manner, or to the threatened reduction in rates.

"It has been said", continued the petition, "that an Indian mill operative is not as hard working as an English workman and that a mill operative in England does the work of three men employed in the same work in an Indian mill. The real cause of this is the bad machinery and bad material used in mills. It is true that three men are required to manage the machine in Indian factories, but these three men, it should be borne in mind, do their work for longer hours without intermission in a more enervating climate and on poorer wages. The operatives in Indian factories have to perform their tasks without many facilities afforded in England and calculated to lessen the burden of workmen and to preserve their constitution against breakdown. The breakage in the thread, for instance, is so continuous here on account of the bad quality of cotton, that millowners are compelled to employ more men. If the cotton were of good quality and the concessions, which were given in England were granted here, one man could manage a machine as well as an English operative."

The claims for compensation for accidents, the petition said, were made in the interests of humanity. The distress brought about upon persons being maimed for life, or even for a few months, was apalling, and some relief to mitigate the sufferings and hardships seemed needed, and the petition asked whether the amount of fines and forfeited wages could not advantageously and with propriety be appropriated for this humane purpose. The necessity for a provision of this character had already been recognized in some mills, where sufferers were adequately provided for. Among the people not yet alive to the advantages of provident funds and mutual benefit societies, some arrangement affording relief to the injured was much needed.

The petition finally prayed that the interest of operatives should be carefully watched in the course of the amendment of the Factory Act of 1881.

Introduction of the Bill into the Legislature.

In the meantime, the Government of India prepared a draft bill in accordance with the advice of the dispatch of the Secretary of State on May 14, 1889. The Secretary of State gave his approval to the bill on January 14, 1890,[60] and a motion was made in the Legislative Council of India, on January 31, 1890, for its introduction.

In moving for leave to introduce the bill, Mr. A. R. Scoble said that the provisions for the Act of 1881 were limited strictly to those points for which legislation had been shown to be necessary, and the provisions of the proposed measure also embodied only those additions and alterations which had been proved to be desirable through the experience of about a decade. Referring to the report of the Factory Commission of 1884, to the statement of Mr. Jones, and to the various questions asked in the House of Commons regarding Indian factory labor, Mr. Scoble said that the extension of the English factory acts to India was quite inexpedient, as stated by the Government of India in the dispatch of March 5, 1885, to the Secretary of State. In accordance with this opinion and taking into consideration the various suggestions made and the evidence submitted, the bill was prepared with eight proposals:

(1) To extend the operation of the act to factories in which not less than 20 persons were employed.

(2) To raise the minimum age at which children might be employed in any factory from 7 to 9 years.

[60] Gt. Brit. Parl. Papers, 1890—91, Vol. 59, H. of C. 224, p. 2.

(3) To limit the hours of employment for women to 11 per day.

(4) To secure to women as well as to children proper intervals for food and rest during the day, and not less than four holidays in each month.

(5) To secure a proper supply of water for the use of operatives.

(6) To insure proper ventilation and cleanliness in factories.

(7) To prevent overcrowding which might be injurious to the health of the operatives.

(8) To give local governments greater power to obtain reports and make rules for the purpose of carying out the objects of the act.

The bill was introduced on the same day.[61]

The bill, as submitted, did not contain any provision for reducing the hours of work for children, which were 9 hours under the existing law, nor attempt to interfere with the hours of work for adult males.

Revival of Agitation in England.

On February 3, 1890, a telegram was sent from Calcutta to the London *Times* epitomizing the proposed factory act for India.[62] Two days later, the Blackburn and District Chamber of Commerce held its annual meeting and discussed the draft bill for Indian factory legislation. On the following day, the secretary of the Chamber wrote a letter to the Secretary of State for India, showing the discrepancies between the proposed Indian factory act and the existing British factory act and requesting him for further and fuller consideration of the matter.[63]

On February 17, 1890, Mr. Samuel Smith, Flint-shire, in the House of Commons, informed the Under Secretary of State for India that great indignation existed among the Lancashire operatives at the competition to which

[61] India, Legislative Council Proceedings, Calcutta, 1890, 29 : 19.

[62] Gt. Brit. Parl. Papers, 1890—91, Vol. 59, H. of C. 120, p. 3.

[63] *Ibid.*

they were exposed by laborers working 80 hours per week in one part of the Empire, while they were restricted by law to 56 hours, and that the factory managers in Bombay, who had had experience with slavery in South Africa said that such slavery was mild in comparison with that which existed in the factories of Bombay,[64] and that young children were employed 80 hours per week to the extreme detriment of their health. The Under Secretary replied that no child in India could be employed by law for more than 54 hours. Mr. C. Graham, Lanmark, N. W., also asked whether it was in the power of the Under Secretary of State for India to advise the Indian Government to introduce some law where by Her Majesty's subjects in different parts of the Empire should not be reduced to slavery.

On March 13, 1890, the Secretary of State for India, who had already given his approval of the bill, as introduced into the Indian Legislative Council, changed his mind and ordered some further changes. In reply, the Governor General informed the Secretary of State, on March 25, 1890, that he had postponed the bill till the receipt of replies from the local governments and administrative bodies.[65] This sudden postponement of legislation could not but arouse some suspicion, and on July 15, 1890, Sir George Campbell asked in the House of Commons whether or not it was suggested by the Secretary of State.[66]

The International Labor Conference at Berlin.

In the meantime a movement was going on in Western Europe to find a solution to the proplem of the excessive hours and other adverse conditions under which the wage-earning classes suffered through the competition of the more advanced nations for the command of the world's market. Switzerland, with that object in view, twice made unsuccessful attempts, first in 1881 and then in

---

[64] Gt. Brit. Parliamentary Debates, 1890, 341 : 1320—22.
[65] Gt. Brit. Parl. Papers, 1890—91, Vol. 59, H. of C. 224, p. 2.
[66] Gt. Brit. Parliamentary Debates, 1890, 346 : 1720.

1889,[67] to reach a common understanding among different advanced countries. At last, Germany became interested in the idea, and on February 8, 1890, Prince Bismark made a proposal to the several nations of Western Europe that they join in an International Labor Conference at Berlin,[68] the principal object of which should be to bring about "an agreement among various governments to obviate the common dangers by the adoption of general measures of prevention".[69] The less advanced nations were, of course, to join the conference for the sole satisfaction of having taken part in a civilizing work,[70] as M. Villori Ellena, Deputy Councillor of State and Delegate from Italy at the conference, put it.

Accordingly the conference was convened at the Palace of the Imperial Chancellor at Berlin from March 15 to March 29, 1890, under the presidentship of Baron de Berlepsch, German Minister of Commerce and Industry. There were representatives from 15 States and the Vatican.[71] Great Britain was represented by Sir John Gorst, Under Secretary of State for India, Mr. Charles S. Scott, C. B., Minister at Berne, and other two ordinary and four expert delegates.

The subjects of discussion in the conference were grouped under six heads: Labor in mines, Sunday labor, child labor, labor for youths, female labor, and the means of putting into force the provisions to be adopted by the conference. The work of drawing up provisional resolutions was entrusted to the different commissions appointed by the conference.

Regarding labor in mines, it was resolved to fix the minimum age at which a person could enter a mining career at 14 years, in order that he might have time to acquire a sufficient physical and intellectual development.[72]

---

[67] Gt. Brit. Parl. Papers, 1890, Vol. 81, C. 6042, p. 9.

[68] Ibid., C. 5914, p. 1.

[69] Ibid., C. 6042, p. 10. Presidential Speech.

[70] Ibid., p. 42.

[71] Germany, Austria, Hungary, Italy, Switzerland, France, Spain, Portugal, Great Britain, Belgium, Netherlands, Luxemburg, Denmark, Sweden and Norway.

[72] Gt. Brit. Parl. Papers, 1890. Vol. 81, C. 6042, p. 51.

At the request of the delegates from Spain and Italy, where the legal age limits were 9 and 10 years respectively, the minimum age was fixed at 12 years for Southern Europe. England declared, however, that she could not take the responsibility of depriving the children of those countries of the benefit to be derived from raising the age limits to 14 years.[73]

In the discussion in connection with Sunday labor, M. Ellena, Italian delegate, said that the countries which had almost completed laws for the protection of labor, made hardly any concessions when they consented to invest their laws with an international character, and that, on the other hand, those countries, which undertook to pass new laws in order to introduce more effectual protection hereafter, made real concessions. Whatever might be the scope of the international agreement which was being proposed, it was impossible to imagine that all countries represented at the conference could have uniform laws of labor; for

(1) the physical and intellectual development of working classes depended on climate, race, etc.

(2) According to the principles which governed public law in different countries, the legislation in question must be confined to the protection of children; otherwise it might be applied also to the regulation of the work of adult men and women.

(3) There were certain industries, notably silk spinning in Italy, which, competing as they did with countries which were not represented at the conference, and in which the conditions of labor were very primitive, could not, without considerable reservation, be made subject to an international agreement.[74]

Regarding Sunday labor, the conference resolved that it was advisable to grant one weekly day of rest, which should be on Sunday to all work people. Exceptions were made in the case of continuous industries and seasonal

---

[73] Gt. Brit. Parl. Papers, 1890, Vol. 81, C. 6042, p. 52.

[74] Ibid., pp. 42—53.

occupations, where one day of rest for every two weeks should be granted.[75]

M. Jules Simon, president of the commission on child labor, proposed to fix the minimum age for admission into factories at 12 years. Mr. Scott, the English delegate, said that there was progressive diminution of the employment of children under 12 years in England, especially in textile industries, but English legislation allowed the employment of children from 10 to 12 under certain restrictions, and gave his vote *ad referendum* in favor of the proposal.[76] M. Boccardo, the Italian delegate, said that the age for admission of children into factories might not be the same for all countries. Geographically, Italy was differently situated and her silk industry competed with the extra European countries of China and Japan. Italy had, therefore, the right to demand a special treatment. "The position of Italy is quite different", argued M. Boccardo, "from that of other States represented at the conference, not only because of the natural development of labor laws, but also on account of the geographical, demographical, and economic conditions of the different countries. On this head, it is evident that the population of Italy cannot be subjected to the same rules as the people of Northern Europe. One must consider, first of all, the precocity of the southern races due to the effect of climate, to their geographical situation, and to the race itself; to fix the same limit of age for admission to factories in all countries, and to settle the protective action of the State over children and youths everywhere in the same way, would be losing the principle of equality, as far as industrial legislation is concerned, which it is the object of the conference to uphold, and imposing stronger restrictions on the southern countries than on the

[75] Gt. Brit. Parl. Papers, 1890, Vol. 81, C. 6042, p. 181. The legal prohibition of work on Sundays existed only in Germany, England and Switzerland, while other countries prohibited Sunday labor only for youths under 16 and girls under 21. Some countries did not allude to Sunday work, but restricted work to six days in the week.

[76] *Ibid.*, p. 60.

northern. Moreover, the manufacturing industry of Italy is still in its infancy; it is far from having attained the degree of development of the great productive countries of Europe. Under these circumstances there could be no question of exacting from Italy a legislation similar to that which protects the interests of the children and young people in other countries".[77]

M. Santa Maria, the Spanish delegate, supported the claim of M. Boccardo. The commission then fixed 12 years as the minimum age for admission into factories for northern Europe and 10 years for southern countries.

When the report of the commission was considered at the conference, Sir John Gorst, in the name of the delegation of Great Britain said: — "The delegates of Great Britain are of opinion that the conference should not take on itself the responsibility of admitting that the limit of age, for the work of children in southern countries, be fixed at 10 years. The limit of 12 years has been generally adopted by the conference in consideration of the demands of physical, moral, and intellectual development of the children. It is especially because lesser restrictions would not be sufficient for the necessary primary instruction, nor for the making of good citizens, that these first years of life should be consecrated to education. If the southern countries are of opinion that under their special circumstances it is possible to abridge this time for children, they should themselves adopt measures of this kind, and not put upon the conference the responsibility of an international sanction".[78]

The conference finally decided to take a separate vote on the question. The proposal for 12 years as the minimum age was carried unanimously with the exceptions of three abstentions.[79] The proposal for 10 years as the minimum age for southern countries was passed by a majority of

[77] Gt. Brit. Parl. Papers, 1890, Vol. 81, C. 6042, p. 60.

[78] Ibid., p. 150.

[79] Ibid., p. 151. Denmark, Spain and Switzerland.

eight against two.[80] Five countries abstained from voting.[81]

The second proposition with regard to child labor discussed by the conference was the necessity of having primary education as a condition for admission into factories. The British delegates could not agree to the proposal, for such a provision could be adopted only in an educational measure, and not in a factory act. In support of this attitude, Sir John Gorst said in the conference that by the provision of the British factory act, children were allowed only to work half time in factories, that is, half a day out of 12 hours, or one day only out of every two and make up their studies even while in factories. The resolution was carried by a majority of eleven votes against two.[82]

When the proposition to limit the actual work of children to 6 hours a day with an interval of at least half an hour came up for discussion, the Hungarian and Italian delegates declared themselves in favor of eight hours of work a day, which was in accord with the spirit of their laws. The Belgian delegate could not agree to the fixing of a maximum day's work for children of from 12 to 15 years of age to less than 12 hours divided by intervals of rest of one hour and a half at least. In the Netherlands, the maximum day for children of from 12 to 16 years of age consisted of 11 hours and the Dutch delegate voted against the proposal. So the proposal was passed by 11 against 4.

When this proposal was made in the conference, Sir John Gorst said that British children did not work more than 60 hours in a fortnight in any industry and in the textile industry for 56½ hours only. But it was possible for a child over 13 to acquire before his time the status of a young worker, if he had satisfied the conditions of primary education. The resolution was passed in almost

---

80 Gt. Brit. Parl. Papers, 1890, Vol. 81, C. 6042, p. 151. Great Britain and Switzerland.

81 Ibid., p. 151. Belgium, Denmark, France, Sweden and Norway.

82 Ibid., pp. 151—52. Denmark and Great Britain.

the same way as before by a vote of 11 against three, the Hungarian delegate abstaining from voting.

The fourth proposition before the conference forbade night work and work in dangerous industries in the case of all children.

As regards their protection, young working people were divided into two classes: — Those of from 14 to 16 years of age of either sex, and those of from 16 to 18 years of age of male sex only. The commission proposed to fix 10 years as the period of actual work for young persons of from 14 to 16 years of age and at least two hours of rest. As there was a close connection between the work of young persons and of adults and as both classes began and ended work at the same time, objection was raised to this proposed reduction of work for young persons. Austria wished to have the period of labor fixed at 11 hours, as adults were allowed to work the same period in that country. The Netherlands also desired an 11 hour day and Belgium a 12 hour day. Spain and Italy abstained from voting. Four countries stood for two hours of rest, seven countries including Great Britain for an hour and a half, and two countries for one hour only. The resolution was passed by 10 votes against two, three abstaining from voting. The conference adopted the resolution of the commission.

Against the resolution of work for youths between the ages of 16 and 18 years, a strong protest was raised. But a resolution was at last carried by 8 votes against 6, one abstaining, to the effect that protection be given to this class regarding maximum hours of labor and work at night and in the dangerous industries, and this resolution was also adopted by the conference.

The commission on woman labor fixed the daily period of labor for women at 11 hours to be broken by rests amounting to a total duration of at least two hours. Mr. Scott, the British delegate, proposed a 10 hour day for women, stating that the system was in force in Great Britain and that she reserved the right to abide by it. "Should the commission not accept it", added Mr. Scott, "or should it not fix the day's work at a maximum of 10 hours, the

British delegate would agree to 11 hours".[83] M. Boccardo, the Italian delegate, raised objection to the definite limitation of work for women above 12 years of age. The only thing possible in this case was the fixation of a maximum and a minimum periods. Even girls below 12 years of age should be excluded from any definite limitation, he argued, when employed in trades, which like silk industry, required a longer working day at particular seasons. Germany and Austria contended for an 11 hour day under the existing state of manufacture and the existing social conditions. The necessity of exceptions regarding seasonal occupations was admitted by Germany.

In the conference, the resolution for an 11 hour day was carried by a vote of 9 against 2 including Belgium and Italy; Denmark, Spain, Hungary and Portugal abstained. Great Britain while voting in the affirmative, regretted that the resolution was not of a sufficiently protective character. The resolution prohibiting night work was passed by a vote of eight against five, while Denmark and Sweden abstained. The period of rest was reduced to an hour and a half, exceptions to be made in certain industries. Women were also prohibited from going to work for four weeks after childbirth.

Several resolutions were also passed regarding the execution of the prohibition adopted by the conference. But the power of the conference did not extend beyond the expression of opinion, the underlying principle of which was given out by the president of the conference himself. "Each country should give to the working classes", said he, "either by legislation or by custom, all that is not incompatible with security of existence for, and development of, national industry, on which the well-being of the workmen depends".[84]

Fresh Agitation in England.

After the Berlin conference, Manchester interests found a new basis of agitation. This time not only the cause of humanity but also the honor of Great Britain, as a

[83] Gt. Brit. Parl. Papers, 1890, Vol. 81, C. 6042, p. 72.
[84] Ibid., p. 78.

signatory to the resolutions of the conference, was shown to be at stake in the matter of the regulation of labor in Indian factories. While some still insisted on the enforcement of British factory law in India, others took the decided position that India must adopt the resolutions of the Berlin conference in the enactment of her factory law. In order that India might faithfully conform to their proposal, they also demanded that the Indian Government should submit the draft of the bill to Parliament before it was introduced into the Legislative Council of India.

"How can this solemn agreement", wrote Mr. J. M. MacLean, referring to the resolution of the Berlin conference on the Sunday holiday, "be forced in Europe, if the Indian rival of the European workman is permitted to go on working seven days in the week instead of six".[85] Mr. Holt. S. Hallett also took up the agitation to enforce the resolution of the Berlin conference on Indian factories, and proposed that Parliament should fully discuss the draft bill of the Indian Government before it was made a law. He thought it would be an absolute disgrace to Great Britain, the acknowledged pioneer of factory legislation in Europe, if Indian manufacturers were still suffered to practise the barbarities which British representatives at the conference fancied themselves able to denounce from a position of unusual security.[86]

On May 5, 1890, Mr. Howorth, Salford, S., asked, in the House of Commons, whether Her Majesty's Government proposed to take steps to bring Indian factories into conformity with the Berlin standard. On the same day, Mr. Mundella asked whether the proposal of the Indian Government to amend the factory act would be brought to the House of Commons before it was enacted by the Indian Legislative Council.[87]

On July 15, 1890, Sir George Campbell, Kirkcaldy, asked the Under Secretary of State for India in the House of Commons whether owing to the fact that the Berlin

---

[85] The Times, London, April 5, 1890, p. 4, c. 3.
[86] Ibid., April 2, 1890, p. 8, c. 2, and April 10, 1890, p. 6, c. 4.
[87] Gt. Brit. Parliamentary Debates, 1890, 344:145—46.

conference was held primarily for European States and, even in that case the southern countries were given concessions, the case of still more southern tropical and semitropical non-European and non-christian countries was considered at the conference; if not, whether the Government of India would be left free to deal with the matter with reference to the situation and feelings of the Indians without being hampered by the example of European countries.[88] On August 14, 1890, Sir George Campbell again took up the question in the House of Commons. "The principles affirmed at the Berlin conference", said Sir John Gorst, the Under Secretary of State for India, in reply, "are being, and will be, observed in India".[89]

In the meantime, Lancashire manufacturers themselves were not inactive. On April 5, 1890, the Secretary of the Blackburn and District Chamber of Commerce again addressed a letter to the Secretary of State for India, in which the Chamber urged: — (1) That under the amended law the hours of work for women and young persons and children would be very much longer in India than in England; (2) That the temperature in Indian factories was more trying than that in English factories; (3) That in the discussion and during the legislation on the subject, the views of employers chiefly had been heard; (4) That the Indian operatives were unable to combine and make their views felt; (5) That it was, therefore, more incumbent on the Government of India to consider the interest of laborers, and that a number of authorities more or less conversant with the question had reported that the hours of labor in Indian factories were too long for women and children, if not for men. According to the Chamber, the proposed amendments to the Indian factory act were framed without consideration for the well-being of the operatives. "It (the Chamber) cannot too strongly express its opinion", concluded the letter, "that in the matter of factory acts, there should not be one law for England and another for India, but that the Indian operatives

[88] Gt. Brit. Parliamentary Debates, 1890, 346:1720.

[89] Ibid., 348:968.

should receive in full the same protection which is granted to their fellow operatives in England".[90]

On May 15, 1890, the Secretary of State for India sent a copy of the correspondence with the Blackburn and District Chamber of Commerce to the Government of India. "As the bill is still under discussion", added the Secretary of State, "the considerations urged in the enclosed papers will have to be weighed by your Excellency's Government and by the legislature."[91] A suggestion was also made for the appointment of a commission consisting principally of Indians with an intelligent operative among its members, which should visit some of the factory centers in order to ascertain the views of factory workers and submit a report for the consideration of the Indian Government and the legislature. In this dispatch the Secretary of State also laid down the following principle upon which the Indian legislation should be based: "The general principle of all factory legislation, as already adopted in this country and in India, is that life and limb must be protected, and that the health of all women, young persons and children, must, so far as possible, be assured. To this principle Her Majesty's Government have recently, in the Berlin conference, declared their adhesion, thus recommending it for adoption by other powers of Europe. How far this general principle has already been applied in India is a matter for your consideration. As regards any additional factory legislation in India, due regard must be had to the circumstances of that country, which are in many respects different from those of any European nation. But the same general principle is nevertheless applicable and the object of any such legislation must be to secure without fail for the various classes of operatives in India, an amount of protection for life and limb and an amount of security for the health of women, young persons, and children not inferior to that which is afforded by the law of England".[92]

---

[90] Gt. Brit. Parl. Papers, 1890—91, Vol. 59, H. of C. 120, p. 7.

[91] Ibid., p. 2.

[92] Ibid., pp. 2—3.

On July 3, 1890, the Secretary of State forwarded the proceedings of the Berlin conference to the Government of India. About the middle of August,[93] the Government of India referred the bill to the local governments for their opinion in connection with the resolutions of the Berlin conference and, by the end of the month,[94] decided to appoint a commission to inquire into factory conditions.

Counter-Agitation in India.

While such agitation was going on in England, India was not free from similar movements, but most of the activities in India were started to offset the agitation of Manchester interests and to preserve India's interests against their rivalry. Public opinion throughout the country was strongly opposed to the bill.[95] The strongest opposing body in India was the manufacturers. They were opposed to any further stringency regarding factory legislation, especially as it was being imposed on India by the British manufacturing interests. Early in April of 1890, the Calcutta Trades Association addressed the Government of Bengal on the subject of the proposed bill pending before the Indian Legislative Council. Its members complained that no information had been given them as to the necessity of the proposed legislation. They objected to the clause raising the age at which children could be employed and maintained that children were invariably given work of the lightest description. They also pointed out that children were brought to factories by their parents, who were not likely to overtax their capabilities. As regards the regulation of women's work, they stated that women were not overworked in factories nor did they need more protection than their sisters in other occupations. Strongly deprecating any measure that might injure the manufacturing industry of India, they prayed

---

[93] The Times, London, Aug. 15, 1890, p. 3, c. 1. Calcutta telegram of Aug. 14.

[94] Ibid., Aug. 29, 1890, p. 3, c. 1. Calcutta telegram of Aug. 28.

[95] Ibid., April 7, 1890, p. 3, c. 3, and April 21, 1890, p. 5, c. 4.

the Lieutenant Governor to recommend the withdrawal of the bill.[96]

Two weeks later, the Bengal Chamber of Commerce, the Calcutta Hydraulic Press Association and the Indian Jute Manufacturers' Association also protested against the bill. Criticising in detail its provisions, they intimated that the restrictions on the work of women and children would result in their elimination from factories and in the employment of men in their place. The proposals for compulsory holidays were not workable and not necessary, because a system of shifts existed and the operatives were accustomed to taking a long vacation every year or every 18 months.[97] On July 24, 1890, the Upper India Chamber of Commerce also protested against legislation on European lines, as it would likely hamper the Indian manufacturing industry.[98]

Workers' Agitation for Amendment.

Side by side with the manufacturers in India, who protested against the attempt of Manchester interests to enforce British factory law and the resolution of the Berlin conference on India, and who, therefore, very often minimised the existence of any grievances on the part of the employees, philanthropists were also working, as before, for the amendment of the Indian factory law and were striving to bring about the real issue between employers and the employees. This time, they organized an association, called the "Millhands' Association". Mr. N. M. Lokhanday, who was the moving spirit of the agitation among the laborers in Bombay and was working in conjunction with Mr. Bengalee, became its president and Mr. D. C. Athaide, its secretary. Mr. Lokhanday also started a paper, called the *Dinabandhu*, or friend of the poor.[99]

---

[96] The *Times*, April 7, 1890, p. 3, c. 3.
[97] *Ibid.*, April 21, 1890, p. 5, c. 3—4.
[98] *Ibid.*, July 25, 1890, p. 5, c. 2.
[99] The association did not have any regular membership and Mr. Lokhanday acted only as an advisor to the employees, whenever they sought his advice, and took an active part in the betterment of their condition.

The most important activity of the philanthropists at this time was a mass meeting of factory employees numbering upwards of 10,000 persons, held at Bombay on April 24, 1890. Two women workers addressed the meeting and complained of being forced to work on Sundays. A memorial was sent from the meeting to the Bombay Millowners' Association asking for a weekly holiday.[100]

The Bombay Millowners' Association held a general meeting on June 10, 1890, at which the memorial of the employees was duly considered. The members of the Association came to the conclusion that the mills should be closed for one day in every seven, such day to be Sunday in each week, unless some native festival intervened. when it was to be observed as holiday in lieu of Sunday, and that on the day preceding the weekly holiday, the mills should be closed two hours earlier than on the ordinary working day for the purpose of cleaning machinery.[101] It was, of course, a great victory for the laborers, and especially for Mr. Lokhanday.

The Factory Commission of 1890.

According to the proposal of the Secretary of State, the Governor General of India appointed, on Sept. 25, 1890, a commission to inquire into the conditions of factory labor, with Surgeon Major A. S. Lethbridge, C. S. I., inspector general of jails, Bengal, as president. There were three regular members in the commission, namely, Mr. Sorabjee S. Bengalee, C. I. E., a member of the Factory Commission of 1884, Raja Peary Mohan Mukherjee, C. I. E., a landholder of Bengal, and Mir Muhammad Hussain, assistant director of land records and agriculture, North Western Provinces and Oudh. The commission was assisted by three local members, who did not have the power to prepare or sign the report. The Bombay Presidency was locally represented by Mr. N. M. Lokhanday, president of the Bombay Millhands' Association. Bengal and the North Western Provinces and Oudh were locally

[100] Gt. Brit. Parliamentary Debates, 1890, 344 : 810—11.
[101] Gt. Brit. Parl. Papers, 1890—91, Vol. 59, H. of C. 86, p.. 108.

represented by Babu Rasik Lal Ghose and Mr. Framji Manakji respectively, the latter being a foreman of the Cawnpore Woollen Mills.[102]

The points upon which the commission was to report were as follows: — (a) limitation of woman labor to 11 hours in any one day; (b) creation of a young person class and the definition of the same; (c) limitation of the work of children to 9 hours; (d) holidays for women and children, and the advisability of granting holidays to adults; (e) fixing of a general working day for male adults; (f) laborers' attitude toward compulsory stoppage at midday.

The commission began its work at Bombay on Oct. 4, 1890, and visited Ahmedabad, Cawnpore and Calcutta. It held 28 meetings, visited 34 factories and examined 96 factory operatives, comprising men, women and children. Before the completion of the report, it received an address, dated Nov. 8, 1890, from Mr. Lokhanday, president of the Millhands' Association and the local member of the commission. In this address, Mr. Lokhanday discussed the importance of the amendment of the factory act and asked for the inclusion of several provisions in the proposed amendment of the factory act, which he called "the demands of the Millhands' Association." A summary of the resolutions he sent to the commission was as follows: —

(1) Millhands should get one complete day of rest on Sundays.

(2) The working day should be included within the period from 6 A. M. to 5.30 P. M.

(3) If practicable, one hour's rest should be given during the day, half an hour between 9 and 10 and half an hour at 12 noon; if not, at least fully half an hour's complete rest at 12 noon.

---

[102] Gt. Brit. Parl. Papers, 1890—91, Vol. 59, H. of C. 86, p. 3. The Times, London, Oct. 9, 1890, p. 5, c. 1.

The commercial community was not satisfied with the composition of the commission. The President, a jail inspector, was not an authority on the question of factory labor, while Raja Peary Mohan Mukherji had no commercial experience. Mr. Bengalee was indentified with restrictive measures. The local members were not men of position and influence.

(4) Payment should be made on the 15th of each month, and the suggestion was also made that weekly payment was preferable and would benefit the employees.

(5) Children from 9 to 14 years of age should work half time; from young persons 15 years of age and over, full time might be exacted.

(6) Women should work from 7 A. M. to 5 P. M.

(7) Provision should be made for injured and sick persons. A suitable dispensary should be attached to every mill and a school should be maintained by every mill for the education of the children employed therein, in case they were permitted to work one half time.

"If the above points are fairly attended to," concluded Mr. Lokhanday, "in the factory act now to be amended, I think the millhands will have no cause to complain".[103]

The report of the commission, which was submitted on November 12, 1890, consisted of the following recommendations: — (1) The proposed limitation of working hours of women to 11 a day was proper and sufficient. Woman workers were found generally in textile factories. They were employed with moving machinery to any appreciable extent only in jute mills, where the work was done in shifts and did not exceed 9 or 10 hours a day. In cotton industries, about 80 per cent of the female employees were reelers and winders, working 11 hours a day. The remaining 20 per cent of the women working with moving machinery were liable to overwork. But in Bengal, owing to the shift system, the working hours of even such women were less than 11 hours.

While proposing the limitation of working hours of women to 11, the commission recommended that exception should be made of the women who were working with moving machinery at Ahmedabad; otherwise they were liable to be replaced by male operatives. The reasons for such fear on the part of the commission were that factory owners did not want to diminish the hours of work for the whole factory and the difference in wages between male and female workers was in most cases small. In support of its

[103] Gt. Brit. Parl. Papers, 1890—91, Vol. 59, H. of C. 86, p. 110.

recommendations, the commission cited the resolution of the Berlin conference, making exceptions for certain industries even in Europe. Mr. Bengalee, who was not present at the Ahmedabad meetings, did not agree with the majority of the commission regarding such exceptions, on the ground that it would lead to the spreading of the evil to other parts of India and result in the procrastination of the administration of the law. He argued that female operatives did not desire the present hours shortened; on the contrary, most of them were strongly against any interference which might subject them to the risk of losing their means of livelihood.

(2) The commission after careful consideration recommended that there should not be any young person class recognized by law as such and that the difficulty should be met by raising the maximum age of children to 14 years. The existing maximum limit of age for children was so low that it was often impossible to guess accurately the age of a child who might be over 10 and under thirteen. The law was consequently violated and many children were employed as full-timers. Whereas the age of 14 would be more easily known to medical officers due to the signs of approaching adolescence and puberty. The commission supported its recommendation on this point by those of the Factory Commission and Medical Committee of 1884 and by the resolutions of the Bombay Government.

(3)Regarding the hours of work for children, the commission was of the opinion that 9 hours' work except for the shift system was too long. But 9 hours in shifts for 4 days, as in Bengal, could not be considered as overwork. Even 9 hours of work for children working on the shift system would reduce wages. In the mills outside of Bengal, where the shift system did not exist, half time was the only solution of the question. Children should not work in those mills more than 6¾ hours in any one day.

The interval of rest granted to the children under existing law was one hour. In case they were employed for half time, the commission believed there was no necessity for any fixed interval of rest by law. The reasons for such recommendation as given by the commission were: — First, to give an interval of rest to children while the machinery was moving and while other operatives were at work, would be so great an inconvenience to millowners that they would certainly try to dispense with the services of children, or the law would be evaded; second, the commission's inquiry had proved beyond all doubts that it was the practice for Indian operatives of all classes to go out of the factory at odd times for smoking, drinking water, and other purposes, and to stay away from 5 to 15 minutes. The taking of casual intervals of rest was possible in India because more employees were employed than in Europe for the same kind of work.

(4) Women and children should have one holiday in every seven, preferably on Sundays, as should male adults also, except where continuous production was necessary. The reasons for this recommendation of holidays for adult males were: — First, it was the unanimous desire of the operatives. Second, most of the factories gave a weekly holiday and the remaining ones gave at least two holidays every month. Third, the factory commission of 1875 and the minority party of the commission of 1884 as well as the Medical Committee of 1884 had recommended such holidays. Fourth, the mill owners of Bombay had accepted the proposal. This holiday should preferably be on Sunday, for it would give the workers a chance to meet their friends, who were employed on week days. Factories might work on Sunday following a native festival holiday; but if two such holidays occurred in one week, the two following Sundays could not be working days.

(5) Operatives desired that the present working day from daylight to dusk should be continued and there was nothing in the conditions of factory labor which called for more legislative restrictions upon the hours of labor of adult males.

(6) There should be a compulsory stoppage of work for full thirty minutes between hours of 12 and 1 P. M. for all adult male operatives not employed on the shift system. This favor had been asked for by mill operatives in their petition to the government.

The commission also made some minor suggestions for the consideration of factory owners: — First, the Bombay factory operatives should be paid monthly on the 15th of the month following that for which it was due. Second, most of the mills around Calcutta and some in Bombay, Ahmedabad and Cawnpore, provided medical advice and treatment for their operatives and those employers who had not yet adopted this dispensary system, should favorably consider the subject. Third, provident funds for operatives disabled by accident or disease should be established in all factories. In some factories, such a system was already in existence. All fines realized and all wages unpaid for any cause, should be credited to this fund. Fourth, some means of instruction of the children, when they were off work, should also be provided. Local governments and municipalities should meet the owners half way and contribute half the cost of teaching factory children. The expenditure for such purposes would be trifling.

"In conclusion", remarked the commission, "we hope we may be allowed to say that we have been profoundly impressed with the vast and far-reaching benefits which the people of India are deriving from the development and prosperity of the great industries which we have seen in our tour through the country. It would, in our judgment, be a great calamity if by any injudicious recommendations or unnecessary restrictions the prosperity of those industries was endangered".[104]

The report of the commission was very favorably received by the Indian public. While it affirmed the necessity of further legislation for Indian factories, it also conclusively proved that the conditions of factory labor in India were radically different from those in England.[105] Its recommendations somewhat allayed the apprehension which clouded the minds of the Indian manufacturers regarding the outcome of the Manchester agitation. The Indian press throughout the country expressed approval

[104] Gt. Brit. Parl. Papers, 1890—91, Vol. 59, H. of C. 86, p. 16.
[105] The Times, London, Dec. 8, 1890, p. 5, c. 2.

of the report and looked upon it as a crushing retort to what it described as "an interested attempt on the part of the Lancashire millowners to check Indian competition".[106] The Upper India Chamber of Commerce described it as a "fair and impartial review of the evidence".[107] The Bengal National Chamber of Commerce representing the Indian commercial community expressed to the government their hope that no legislation would be undertaken which would endanger the prosperity of the manufacturing interests.[108]

Further Agitation in England.

But the recommendations of the commission were not at all satisfactory to the Manchester interests. Even when the commission was investigating the labor conditions in Indian factories, Mr. Holt S. Hallett wrote an article that appeared in the Times, London, in which he described the evil effects of standing for long periods at factory work on the physique of operatives, especially of youths under eighteen and of women. "I would urge," added Mr. Hallett, "that a surgical examination of the operatives in one of the native factories should be undertaken by a medical committee".[109] Again on October 27, 1890, he urged, as before, in another article that the principles of the Berlin conference should be applied to Indian factories and the bill for Indian factory legislation should be laid upon the table of the House of Commons and debated before it was enacted into law.[110] Sir George Campbell strongly criticised, on November 10, 1890, the last proposal of Mr. Hallett, whom he called the "advocate of Manchester commercial interests." He pointed out that questions between the English interests and those of the Indian people could not be discussed in the House of Commons, where one side was represented and the other side was not. "But it curiously enough happens," observed

[106] The Times, London, Dec. 25, 1890, p. 3, c. 1.
[107] Ibid., Jan. 9, 1891, p. 3, c. 1.
[108] Ibid., Jan. 28, 1891, p. 5, c. 1.
[109] Ibid., Oct. 15, 1890, p. 3, c. 4.
[110] Ibid., Oct. 27. 1890, p. 4, c. 4.

Sir George, "that philanthropic gentlemen who are actively moved in the matter are invariably the representatives of English manufacturing constituencies to whose trade the Indian manufacturers threaten rivalry."[111]

On February 17, 1891, Mr. MacLean, Oldham, disappointed with the recommendations of the commission, asked the First Lord of the Treasury in the House of Commons, for assurances that the Government of India would pass the bill to amend the Indian factory act before the Viceroy left Calcutta for Simla, and that the provision of the bill would include as a minimum the rules adopted by the international labor conference at Berlin regarding age, hours of labor, and hours of rest and refreshment. The First Lord of the Treasury in reply gave the required assurances but said that it had been proposed to fix the minimum age for children at 9 years. Mr. MacLean insisted that as the minimum age for employment of children in some European countries was fixed at 10 years by the conference at Berlin and as Indian children were weaker physically than children in European countries, the Right Hon. Gentleman should impress upon the Indian Government the importance of fixing the minimum age at 10 years instead of at 9. "I have no hestitation in saying," said the First Lord in reply, "that the Secretary of State is impressing that view upon the Government of India, and will continue to do so".[112]

Sir George Campbell asked whether the recommendations of the Berlin conference were applicable to the case of a tropical country, and whether they were consistent with the desire of the people of India or whether they were only urged upon the Government by a few Lancashire members. "I am not aware of the limitation," replied the First Lord of the Treasury, "to which the Honorable Member refers, but I am under the impression that the sole object the Government of India and the Secretary of State have in view is that the regulation of labor in

---

111 The Times, London, Nov. 10, 1890, p. 13, c. 5.

112 Gt. Brit. Parliamentary Debates, 1891, 350 : 844—45.

factories in India is consonant with humanity and in the interests of the Indian people themselves".[113]

Controversy between the Secretary of State for India and the Governor General.

In the meantime the report of the commission was under consideration by the local governments, to which the Government of India had sent it for their opinion. But before all their opinions had been taken into consideration, the Government of India received three cable dispatches between January 23 and February 10, 1891, from the Secretary of State for India urging expedition of its views on the report of the commission and its legislative proposals. On February 12, 1891, the Government received another dispatch from the Secretary of State asking for assurance that the bill would be passed during the session then in progress, and that the act would include as a minimum the rules adopted at the Berlin conference regarding age of employment, hours of labor, and rest and refreshment.[114]

In reply, the Government of India notified the Secretary of State on Feb. 13, 1891, of the following conclusions which had been reached on the report of the factory commission:

(1) Eleven hours' actual work was to be prescribed as the maximum for women, with one hour's interval of rest; in addition, the Government of India was to reserve power to exempt certain industries, as resolved at the Berlin conference, but not individuals, as suggested by the commission.

(2) Nine and 14 were to be fixed as the minimum and maximum ages respectively for children; no separate class of young persons was to be made for reasons indicated by the commission.

(3) Half time work not exceeding the maximum of 7 hours was to be fixed for children defined as half-timers;

[113] Gt. Brit. Parliamentary Debates. 1891, 350 : 844—45.
[114] Ibid., 1891, 356 : 1270.

with this provision in force, no interval of rest for children would be necessary.

(4) Sunday holiday was to be adopted for all factories, excluding continuous industries and seasonal occupations, which would be exempted by the Government of India according to the second resolution of the Berlin conference. Sunday labor was to be allowed only when a native festival was given within the week.

(5) Midday stoppage of half an hour was to be made compulsory in all factories subject to the same exceptions as Sunday labor.[115]

On Feb. 17, 1891, the Secretary of State informed the Government of India that the resolutions of the Berlin conference had a great weight with Her Majesty's Government and had attracted increasing attention, and in accordance with the recommendation made by that conference he insisted (1) that children's actual hours of work should be 6 with half an hour's interval of rest, (2) that women's interval of rest should be extended from one hour to one and a half, and (3) that employment of women and children at night should be prohibited, but this need not prevent work in cool hours of early morning. Finally, the Secretary of State also asked the Governor General whether he was satisfied that the minimum age for children at 9 instead of at 10 was safe and in accordance with the views of employees.

The Government of India in reply, on Feb. 20, 1891, informed the Secretary of State for India that in its opinion the conclusions, stated in the reply of Feb. 13, followed the resolutions of the Berlin conference as far as was reasonable, due regard being had to the difference in the conditions between India and Europe. The Government was, however, prepared to accept the second and the third modifications, regarding the period of rest for women and night work for women and children. "We must strongly object," continued the Governor General, "to your modifications of our conclusions relating to hours and interval

[115] Gt. Brit. Parl. Papers, 1890—91. Vol. 59, H. of C. 224, p. 3.

of rest for children. Anything less than half time according to season will very prejudicially affect the mills".[116] In support of its position, the Government of India pointed out that casual absences were allowed in all Indian factories, that such a modification was uncalled for and would give rise to great dissatisfaction in the country. Moreover, so great a change in the bill at that time would necessitate further consultations with interested bodies and would thus result in the postponement of the bill for the session. The Government of India further showed that the Berlin conference, according to the resolutions of which the Secretary of State tried to regulate the hours of labor in India, provided 10 hours for young persons between 14 and 16 years of age. As 12 and 14 in India corresponded repectively to those ages in Europe, the Government decided not to create any separate young person class. "If, therefore, your Lordship's proposal as to hours for children is pressed," affirmed the Governor General, "we shall have to reconsider our decision as to young persons." To the last question of the Secretary of State, the Government replied that the minimum age of 9 in India corresponded with 10 in southern Europe and that it was safe and in accordance with the wishes of factory laborers.

In the dispatch of Feb. 21, 1891, the Secretary of State for India insisted on the statutory recognition of the interval of rest for children and on the passing of this bill in the same session. "Her Majesty's Government," asserted the Secretary of State, "have considered your telegram of the 20th instant and have decided that bill must be proceeded with and passed this session wihout fail".[117] On February 24, 1891, the Government of India accepted the order with the condition that such an interval of rest for half-timers would be so arranged as not to necessitate the stoppage of machinery. On the same day, the Secretary of State approved of this modification.

On March 6, 1891, the report of the select committee on factory bill was submitted to the Legislative Council of India. The principal amendments proposed were: —

---

[116] Gt. Brit. Parl. Papers, 1890—91, Vol. 59, H. of C. 224, p. 4.
[117] Ibid.

(1) Any factory employing 50 persons should come under the act. Local governments were to be empowered to extend this measure even to a factory where only 20 persons were employed.[118]

(2) The minimum and maximum ages of children were to be fixed at 9 and 14 years respectively.

(3) All operatives were to enjoy complete rest on Sundays; unless a holiday intervened during three days before or after, when the work should be done on the previous or following Sunday.

(4) The labor of women was restricted to 11 hours and to the period between 5 A. M. and 8 P. M. except where the shift system was enforced. They should get one and a half hours' rest for every 11 hours' work or a proportionate rest for a less amount of work.

(5) Factories not worked on the shift system must stop for half an hour at midday.

(6) Children were only to be employed for 7 hours unless in shifts when they might work two shifts of 4 hours each, provided that an interval of two hours was given. Children were not to be employed under any circumstances between 8 P. M. and 5 A. M. An interval of, or intervals aggregating to, at least half an hour, was to be given to children working for 6 consecutive hours.

On March 7, 1891, the Government of India informed the Secretary of State of the two following important changes made in the bill:[119] —

(1) Women were permitted to work at night when work was arranged on the shift system. Night work was uncommon, but where it prevailed, the Government saw no reason to debar women from it. In hot weather it was less fatiguing and the people in India were accustomed to sleep at any hour.

(2) Where the shift system prevailed, children were allowed to work two shifts, each not exceeding four hours, with minimum intervals of two hours.

---

[118] This provision was made to enable the Bombay Government to bring within the act the small ginning establishments which were reported to be in objectionable condition.

[119] Gt. Brit. Parl. Papers, 1890—91, Vol. 59, H. of C. 224, p. 5.

According to the Indian Government these concessions were fair and consistent with the health of the operative and essential for the passing of the bill immediately.

In reply, the Secretary of State, on March 9, 1891, did not object to the permission of night work for women, provided the actual hours of work did not amount to more than 11 hours in any one day and that one hour and a half of rest was granted. Regarding the second concession, the Secretary of State affirmed that Her Majesty's Government could not agree to any such modifications; but children could work two shifts of four hours with intervals of two hours, and one shift of four hours on alternate days, provided no child's labor exceeded 12 hours in any two consecutive days.[120]

Passage of the Bill.

On March 19, 1891, the factory amendment bill was finally taken into consideration by the Indian Legislative Council. It was the result of three sets of recommendations, viz., those of the Bombay Factory Commission of 1884, those of the Berlin Labor Conference of 1890, and those of the Indian Factory Commission of 1890, and, as such, was materially different from the original bill, which was formulated on the recommendation of the Commission of 1884 only and introduced on January 31, 1890. The point was, therefore, raised whether the opinion of the local governments and commercial bodies should not be secured before it was taken up for final consideration by the council. It was pointed out in the course of discussion that though the select committee on the bill was appointed about a year before, its services were not called into requisition until the second of March, 1891, and that the report of the select committee was not published until

[120] This final telegram was sent as urgent under the Section 26 of the 21 and 22 Victoria Chapter 106, which makes provision for urgent cases. This provision empowers the Secretary of State in extreme urgency to override the opinion of the Government of India and also of the members of the Indian Council. Parl. Debates, 1891, 356 : 1268. See also Gt. Brit. Parl. Papers, 1890--91, Vol. 59, H. of C. 224, p. 5.

the 7th of March; that is, 13 days before the bill was taken up by the council. Distant parts of the country had not had sufficient time to express their opinion. In reply Mr. P. P. Hutchins, C. S. I., said for the Government that the main provisions of the bill had been telegraphed all over the country immediately after its publication and the opinion of all parties concerned had been secured.

The chief points at issue in connection with the provisions of the bill were the increased stringency on child labor and the introduction of restriction on woman labor. As regards child labor, the main objection was raised against the provision that a child employed continuously for six hours must have half an hour's interval of rest. The objection was based on the following arguments: — First, such compulsory rest was unnecessary in consideration of the fact that children henceforward were going to be half-timers. Second, it would not be possible to grant them such a leave of absence from moving machinery at which they were generally employed. This provision would only serve to militate against the employment of children in factories, and be, therefore, injurious.

In reply, the government pointed out that this was not a novel feature in the provision; for the act, then in force, allowed one hour's rest for 9 hours' work, which, if maintained in the same proportion, would give 45 minutes instead of 30 for 6 hours' work. Where such interval was already in use, it would not be hard to adjust the work in rotation, or otherwise, for the stated intervals. Moreover, all employees were accustomed to taking occasional leave of absence for a few minutes, even though employed on moving machinery, and there were always some extra hands to meet such cases. Neighbors were also always ready to help one another. The new provision only made statutory recognition of the existing practice. Regarding the provision for barring children from night work, the government said that children had never worked at night and it was better that they should not start doing so.

The most important feature of the bill, as indicated above, was the provision for the regulation of woman labor in factories. Three members of the council compared the labor of women in the field and in the factory and showed that the work of the latter was much easier and more remunerative than that of the former. In the field, the women had to work longer hours, at times in rain and at times in the burning sun. Mr. H. W. Bliss, Madras, official member, said that, owing to higher wages earned in the factory, there had been created new wants and higher standards of comfort among female employees. Mr. J. Nugent, official member, objected to the limitation of the hours of labor for women to 11 by legislation, though they actually did not work longer hours. It interfered with a woman's exercise of her own discretion and the disposition of her own labor. But his stronger objection was to the prolonged compulsory grant of intervals of rest, amounting to one hour and a half for every 11 hours of work. This he insisted went beyond the recommendation of the factory commission and was drafted from the resolutions of the Berlin conference. The effect of this provision would be: — The decrease of wages of women during the winter months in all the factories except a few where artificial light had been introduced, and stricter discipline which would prove harmful to them. Referring to the fact that the Bombay millowners were willing to accept this provision, Mr. Nugent doubted seriously whether they realized the full significance of its consequences. Mr. Bliss said that if 12½ hours were taken as an average working day, this provision would shorten women's work by one hour in comparison with men's. The question which he raised was how far it would result in the disorganization of the industry. Mill owners agreed to the provision on the belief that they would be able to dispense with the services of female tenders of moving machinery. Mr. J. L. Mackay, president of the Bombay Chamber of Commerce, said that if an act were passed to this effect, it would certainly drive many women from factory labor and result in disaster to them. They earned four times as much in the factory as in the field. "As regards the relative hardships of the two conditions of labor," added Mr. Mackay, "I feel sure if a Lancashire philanthropist had to choose between working on the roads under an April sun and tending a spinning frame in the shelter of a factory, he would rapidly run from the road and make for the mill".[121]

Discussing the question of night work for women, Mr. Nugent pointed out that in cotton gins and presses, it would be found disastrous to exclude women from night labor during the busy season, when the work must be done within a definite time. This period of work was short and no harm could arise from such seasonal work, though the hours were rather long. Mr. G. H. Evans, non-official member, said that conception of night in Europe differed from that in India. Work requiring little light was more congenial at night in India than during the day.

In reply, the government said that the 11 hour day would not affect more than 20 per cent of woman factory workers. This would not apply to Bengal where the shift system was in force. The provision was based on the recommendation of the factory commission and might be taken as unanimously agreed upon. The government admitted that the interval of rest had been raised from one hour to one hour and a half following the resolution of the Berlin conference. But 11 hours' work with a period of rest for an hour and a half would constitute a 12½ hour working day, usually found in factories. Under this arrangement, women could attend and leave factories at the same time as the men, the only essential point being to arrange the work so as to give them the appointed rest. Generally two persons worked together, as at Ahmedabad, and one of them could easily take leave for some time and they generally did take such periodical spells of rest. What difference would it make, if such intervals were arranged for beforehand?

One of the most irritating points in connection with the proposed act was the attempt on the part of the officials in the India Office and of the Manchester interests to impose on India the resolutions of the Berlin conference. Almost all the members deprecated it on the ground that

[121] India, Legislative Council Proceedings, Calcutta, 1891, 30 : 161.

India was not represented at the conference at least not directly, that no representative who attented the conference had any practical knowledge of India and of her conditions of labor, and that conditions in Asia and in Europe were quite different. It was pointed out that the one and a half hour's compulsory interval of rest for women had been adopted from the resolutions of the Berlin conference. But the protocol of the conference had never been laid before the public of India in such a way as to invite attention, or to raise suspicion, that their essence would be incorporated in the factory law of India. "I must lodge a protest," said Rao Bahadur Krishnaji Lakshman Nulkar, C. I. E., non-official Indian member, "at the attempt which appears to have been made by Parliament through the India Office to force on India some of the conclusions of the Berlin conference, which had exclusive reference to European conditions, and in arriving at which Indian interests have not been properly represented".[122]

The most heated part of the discussion on the bill was centered on the origin of the measure. All the members, official and non-official, referred more or less plainly to the belief, which prevailed throughout the country, that the bill was introduced not because that there was any proven necessity for it, but because it was demanded by Lancashire manufacturers.

Mr. Mackay remarked that there had been for the past years a sense of insecurity caused by the feeling that there was a risk that interests of India were being sacrificed on the altar of English party politics. It had again been brought to their recollection by the fact that not long before the Indian import duties were abolished for the benefit of Lancashire manufacturers and replaced by a direct tax upon income entirely unsuited to the conditions of the country, and it was apprehended that Lancashire influence and Oldham agitation might again carry the day.[123]

---

[122] India, Legislative Council Proceedings, Calcutta, 1891, 30 : 179.

[123] Ibid.

Mr. Nugent said that this measure regulating the labor of women and children in factories was only a prelude to the imposition of further restrictions which would result in the exclusion of all women and of nearly all children from employment on moving machinery, as feared by the commission. The interests of another class of people who, at a great risk and by investment of millions of pounds sterling, had built new industries, adding immense wealth to the country and providing means of livelihood to thousands of poor people, should also be taken into consideration. "We should, I think," concluded Mr. Nugent, "protect the Indian operative within all reasonable limits, but we should not protect out of existence him and the industry which is his livelihood, nor should the protection of the Indian mill-hand be converted into a device for the protection of the British manufacturer against the Indian mill-owner".[124]

Rao Bahadur Krishnaji Lakshman Nulkar expressed the opinion that the British philanthropists could not expect India to believe that their feelings of humanity were really shocked at the hardships under which the Indian factory laborers worked when they imposed the measure for their speedy removal; for not long ago the same philanthropists had worked successfully for the abolition of the cotton duties and thereby compelled the Government of India to enhance the salt duty to make up the financial deficit. And he suggested that the Government should publish unreservedly the entire official correspondence between England and India and let the people solve their doubts on a matter which had caused so much irritation all over the country.

Mr. Bliss drew the attention of the council to the general question of Indian factory legislation, the impulse for which was undoubtedly not indigenous but came from England. He was not afraid of being guilty of injustice to some of those who professed anxiety to save Indian operatives from oppression and overwork, if he suggested

---

[124] India Legislative Council Proceedings, Calcutta, 1891. 30 : 171.

that, in some cases, the underlying motive of that impulse was the hope that restriction imposed on Indian factory labor would lead to the profits of the mill owners and operatives of Lancashire. "My Lord", concluded Mr. Bliss, "I venture to think that this is a matter on which there should be a very clear understanding, the use of the words "as a minimum" foreshadows an attempt to force upon the manufacturing industries of India restrictions which are absolutely unnecessary for the protection of the operatives and the effect of which must be the serious injury, if not extinction, of the work to which they are applied. The present situation of India in this respect appears to me to be ominously like that of Ireland at the end of the seventeenth century. In both cases we have a subject agricultural country seeking to establish manufactures which will compete with the manufactures of the country which has subjected it. Let us hope that the parallel may not be carried further, and that England may not bring disgrace upon herself by suppressing the cotton and jute industries of India as she suppressed the woollen industries of Ireland".[125]

In support of the bill, the Governor General said that the proposals had been framed with an earnest desire to hold the balance fairly between the interests of Indian industry and the demands which had been made for even stricter regulation of the conditions of Indian factory labor. It was absolutely necessary for the government to effect a settlement of the matter in a way that might be acceptable both in India and in England. "We believe," added His Excellency, "that the effect of our measure will be to place factory labor in India on a proper footing, and that our bill will be accepted here and at home, not, as the Hon. Mr. Nugent would have us believe, as a mere "prelude" to still further restrictions, but as a settlement as final as any settlement of such a question can be."[126]

---

[125] India, Legislative Council Proceedings, Calcutta, 1891. 30 : 177.

[126] Ibid., 30 : 192.

With some minor amendments, the bill was passed on the same day, and the act was called Indian Factories Act, 1891, being Act No XI of 1891, and came into force on January 1, 1892.

Chief Provisions of the Act.

1. The Act included under its jurisdiction all factories employing 50 persons and might be extended to those employing 20 persons at the option of the local governments.

2. The minimum and maximum age limits for the employment of children were raised to 9 and 12 respectively. The certification of their age was made compulsory. Their hours of work were limited to 7 in any one day and to the period between 5 A. M. and 8 P. M. only with half an hour's interval of rest for every 6 hours' continuous work.

3. The hours of work for women were limited to 11 in any one day and to the period between 5 A. M. and 8 P. M. with an interval of rest of an hour and a half, or proportionately less for less number of hours.

4. All factories had to stop work a full half-hour about midday. There was also a weekly holiday on Sunday or any other substituted day in the week.

5. The local governments were given power to make rules regarding the measures of sanitation and comfort, such as cleanliness, ventilation and water supply.

CHAPTER IV.

FACTORY ACT OF 1911.

Agitation in England for Amendment.

The principal feature of the Factory Act of 1891 was the regulation of the hours of labor for women. The restriction of their work to 11 hours a day and the compulsory interval of rest for an hour and a half had a far-reaching effect. But the immediate effect of this measure was that 259 women were thrown out of the factories of Ahmedabad and other places, where they had been employed in the same kind of work as men, and the wages of the rest were reduced 25 per cent.[1]

As in the case of the first factory act, the provisions of the present act satisfied neither the Manchester interests in England nor the textile interests in India. Philanthropists in both countries were also disappointed. No sooner was the act passed than agitation was started in England to amend it. Two members representing Oldham and Northwest Manchester in the House of Commons, one of them being Mr. MacLean, the foremost agitator for the restriction of labor in Indian factories, decided to await the result of the new act before the renewal of agitation for further restriction.[2] But others, both in and out of Parliament, kept on the agitation for the re-enactment of the act, even before it came into force.

It should be remembered that the British delegates at the Berlin conference advocated 12 years as the minimum age for employment of children in factories and they did so with explicit permission of Lord Salisbury, who was then foreign minister. England pledged herself to conform resolutely to the benevolent principles of the conference. But when the question as to raising the age of British factory children from 10 to 12 years as the minimum requirement for employment arose, the British

[1] Gt. Brit. Parl. Papers, 1894, Vol. 58, H. of C. 108, p. 57.
[2] Gt. Brit. Parliamentary Debates, 1891, 356 : 1277.

Government found it a hard task to maintain the position she had taken and was not, in fact, able to do so. Even some of the champions of the Manchester interests, who, in season and out of season, attempted the enforcement of the resolutions of the Berlin conference on India, stood against the application of the same to England. Mr. MacLean tried to show, on May 7, 1891, in the House of Commons, that the assent given by Her Majesty's Government to the above resolution was only conditional and subject to the right on the part of Great Britain "to make such reservations as special local circumstances, the sentiments of particular classes of the population, and the necessities of special branches of industry may from time to time require".[3] Hon. W. Summers pointed out that the quotation given by Mr. MacLean had nothing to do with the question of raising the age of half-timers, but had reference to an entirely distinct and separate question. Mr. MacLean in reply said that Her Majesty's Government was under no obligation to foreign powers with respect to children employed on the half-time system. For this change in attitude, Mr. MacLean was severely accused of inconsistency. Sir George Campbell remarked that Mr. MacLean objected to applying to Great Britain the very resolution of the Berlin conference, which he had been, from the first, one of the most determined to force upon India. In his attempt to exonerate himself, Mr. MacLean replied that since the India Government did not accept these resolutions, he was perfectly free to act on the question of applying them to Great Britain.[5]

The most prominent agitator outside Parliament was Mr. Holt S. Hallett, who for the past two years, as we have seen, had been writing on the necessity of strict restrictive measures on labor in Indian factories. He was regarded as an authority on the subject and had on several occasions been quoted by other agitators in Parliament.[6]

---

[3] Gt. Brit. Parliamentary Debates, 1891, 353 : 282—4.
[4] Ibid.
[5] Ibid., 1891, 356 : 1277.
[6] E. G., by Sir John Gorst, the editor of the *Times*, etc.

On May 20, 1891, he had a long article in the Times, London, severely criticising the new Indian factory act, which did not extend to seasonal employments nor protect workers in factories employing fewer than 50 hands. "Even in factories working through the year and employing over 50 persons," wrote Mr. Hallett, "girls above 14 years of age are classed as women notwithstanding that Mrs. Pechey Phipson, who for the last seven years has medically attended native Indian females, declared, in her recent lecture delivered in Bombay, that a Hindoo girl of 15 is about equal to an English girl of 11 instead of the reverse, and that statements to the contrary by Englishmen who had no opportunity of being acquainted with Hindoo family life were totally misleading. It is very difficult to hunt down and exterminate a lie which has been so successfully propagated by persons eager to delude the public. Thus we find the untruth, propagated by the Indian mill owners in their interests, repeated as gospel by the Viceroy in his telegram to Lord Cross, dated February 20, 1891, four months afterward Mrs. Pechey Phipson unmasked it and conclusively proved it to be a falsehood".[7]

Mr. Hallett furthermore complained that the same protection which had been granted by the factory and workshop acts in Great Britain was not accorded to the working classes of India, though a resolution had been unanimously passed by the Associated Chamber of Commerce to that effect on March 3, 1891, and he finally asked the British electors to take up the question in Parliament. "Children under the new Act," continued Mr. Hallett, "are allowed to work 42 hours a week in the large factories and 168 hours a week in small factories and workshops. Lads from 14 to 18 years of age are permitted to work 141 hours a week in the large factories and 168 hours in small factories and workshops. Girls from 14 years of age upwards are classed as women and are permitted to work 66 hours a week in the large factories and 168 hours a week in minor factories and

[7] The Times, London, May 20, 1891, p. 18, c. 1.

workshops. Such legislation is a slur upon the English name and a disgrace to this nation".[8]

On June 26, 1891, Mrs. Phipson wrote a letter from Bombay, which was published in the London Times on July 17 following,[9] criticising Mr. Hallett's use of her speech on the condition of Indian women as a protest against their work in Indian factories. "I have read from time to time," continued Mrs. Phipson, "the letters of your correspondent, Mr. Holt S. Hallett, upon the Indian Factory Act, and have been struck more than once with the small acquaintance with the conditions of Indian factory life displayed in them. But my astonishment reaches a climax on seeing words of mine quoted as an argument against the employment of Indian women in factories. If, as it seems to me, they are slow in reaching physical development, there is all the more reason why they should adopt the comparatively light and easy work of a mill-hand instead of the hard labor of a coolie or of an agricultural laborer".[10] Contrasting the conditions of work under which she had personally seen Indian women undergo extreme hardships either from carrying heavy weights in the scorching rays of the tropical sun or from planting paddy in a field with "their heads in the fire and their feet in the water" with "the quiet, easy, well-paid work of an airy, shady mill," Mrs. Phipson remarked that the recent factory act by making a difference between the hours of work for men and women would compel the manufacturers to oust women from the mills wherever they were employed on moving machinery with men. "Thus," added Mrs. Phipson, "is a cruel wrong about to be inflicted under the guise of English philanthropy."[11]

Finally, on Aug. 4, 1891, Hon. A. D. Provand, Glasgow, Blackfriars, drew the attention of the House of Commons to the insufficient character of the recent Indian Factory Act for removing the abuses in connection with labor in Indian factories. He referred to the rapid growth and

[8] The Times, London, May 20, 1891, p. 8, c. 2.
[9] Ibid., July 17, 1891, p. 14, c. 2.
[10] Ibid.
[11] Ibid.

prosperous condition of Indian factories, which had put employers in a better position to introduce reforms, and mentioned the existence of long hours of factory work and the inadequacy of inspection even under the recent act. On the ground that Indian laboring classes could not protect themselves by combination and that the Indian women, owing to physical weakness, were unable to stand long hours of factory work, Mr. Provand urged the House "to do partial justice to the laboring classes of India"[12] by re-amending the act according to the provisions of the British factory act and the resolutions of the Berlin conference.

The proposal of Mr. Provand was strongly opposed in the House of Commons by Hon. T. R. Buchanan, Edinburg, W., and Sir George Campbell. Mr. Buchanan protested against any intention on the part of the Secretary of State for India to carry out Mr. Provand's proposal and pointed out that the imposition of the provisions of the British factory acts on India would result in the usurpation of the function which had been delegated to the legislative authority of the Governor General and Council and would, therefore, be extremely unfair both to the people and to the Government of India. He referred to the recent Indian factory act, the details of which were settled by instructions from the India office and under protest on several points from the Governor General of India, Regarding the second proposal, Mr. Buchanan said that the decision of the Berlin conference relating to factory legislation had not been carried out by the ministry of which the Secretary of State for India was himself a member. "It would, therefore," concluded Mr. Buchanan, "be altogether inconsistent if Her Majesty's Government were to endeavor to enforce legislation in reference to factory labor in India, while, at the same time, they are not willing to insist on the recommendations of the Berlin conference being adopted in their own country".[13]

Sir George Campbell said that he did not think that any case had been made out regarding atrocities connected

[12] Gt. Brit. Parliamentarv Debates, 1891, 356 : 1260—66.
[13] Ibid., 356 : 1267.

with the work and labor of Indian men, women and children, to which allusion had been made, and that Her Majesty's Government, which very much depend d upon Lancashire votes, had already urged the Government of India to do a great deal more than it was willing to do. The Indian Government had done all that was necessary and it was questionable whether they had not gone a little too far in regard to the women of India. Referring to the possible elimination of women from factories under the new act, he said that it would be an enormous evil to India. "Of all things," continued Sir George, "we should try to bring forward the women of India; to give them an opportunity of getting work at fair wages, and thereby of raising themselves to a higher position in the social scale. Such an opportunity they have been getting in the Indian factories, and it is one which we should endeavor still more to develop. What I say is that at the instigation of jealous Lancashire manufacturers to put any clogs or hindrances on such employment would be to do a very great injury to the people of India."[14]

After this discussion, the agitation of the Manchester party in the House of Commons subsided. Mr. S. Smith, Flintshire, one of the principal agitators, admitted that one of the principal motives of legislative restriction on Indian factory labor was the indignation of the Lancashire operatives at the competition to which they were subjected.[15] "But I could not help considering," declared Mr. MacLean, the leader of the Parliamentary agitation after that act was passed, "that there was a political aspect to this question. We know that the concessions which have been made — and they are very substantial concessions — have been wrung from the Government of India against their will."[16] Commenting on this discussion in the House of Commons, the Times, in its editorial of August 10, 1891, remarked that the narrow escape, which India had again had from wide-spread

---

[14] Gt. Brit. Parliamentary Debates, 1891, 356 : 1274—75.

[15] Ibid., 356 : 1269.

[16] Ibid., 356 : 1277.

starvation might well make the fair-minded Englishman consider whether it would be true philanthropy or political immorality for England to interfere with industries, which fed millions of men, women and children.[17]

But Mr. Hallett carried the matter still further. The seventh International Congress of Hygiene and Demography had its meetings in London from August 10 to 17, 1891. Mr. Hallett brought the question of Indian factory legislation before the section on Indian Hygiene and Demography. He complained that the Indian Government refused protective legislation to the great bulk of the working classes, that children of any age were thus excluded from the operation of the Act and that merciless employers took advantage of their helplessness. "It is surely abominable cruelty," continued Mr. Hallett, "to allow lads, girls, women, and children to be employed in them (cotton presses and gins) day after day for 23½ hours at a stretch."[18] Mr. Hallett asserted that even under the recent Act of the Indian Government lads and men might be employed day and night for six days in the week, or for 144 hours a week without rest, and for 141 hours a week in mills using electric or other artificial light, but not working on the shift system.[19] In support of his view that the age limits of children were too low and the working hours too long, he quoted the opinion of several physicians acquainted with Indian factory conditions and again urged the application of the British factory and workshop act to the Indian Empire so that the "miserably degraded and joyless toilers in dark, dirty, dusky, overcrowded and unwholesome dens", the "puny overtasked natives of India", who were treated "worse than beasts of burden," "slaving as no slave would work,," might be raised from their existing "state of moral and physical degradation and rescued "from the

---

[17] Loc. cit., p. 12, c. 1.

[18] International Congress of Hygiene and Demography, London, 1891. Transactions, Vol. 10, Div. 2 (Demography), p. 221

[19] Ibid.

inhuman exaction of their merciless task masters" who were "wringing the very life out of them.[20]

Mr. K. N. Bahadhurji, M. D., London, professor at the Bombay Grant Medical College and Indian representative at the Congress, read a paper on the conditions of labor in Indian factories, in which he contended:

First, that the hours of work in factories were not too long nor too arduous. The operatives did not work more than 9½ or 10 hours out of the 12 hours and 6 minutes of the average time spent in factories. Owing to habit and constitution, Indian operatives were accustomed to stop work after short spells and over 10 per cent of them were always found outside of the mill. It was thus necessary for them to work longer than English operatives.

Second, that as regards conditions under which work was performed, much could be said in favor of Indian factories. "In point of light, ventilation and breathing space," continued Dr. Bahadhurji, "the mill he (the operative) works in, is much superior to the chamber he lives in."[21] In the open field he said that the Indian laborer worked from sunrise to sunset in all sorts of weather with a temperature ranging from 110 to 160 degrees of heat, while in the mill the temperature was about 95 degrees, and he was protected from the direct rays of the sun. The mill atmosphere in India was free from the degree of moisture which was imparted to the mill-air in England from the use of steam all day long. The Indian mills were more lofty and capacious, giving more breathing space per person than did the generality of English mills. There was also the immense advantage of the Indian sun, which did away with the harmful effect of artificial light.

Third, that the operatives did not show any sign of breakdown in health or physique. The women were particularly healthy and strong as compared with the woman laborers outside the mill. This Dr. Bahadhurji proved from

---

[20] International Congress of Hygiene and Demography, London, 1891, Transaction, Vol. 10, Div. 2 (Demography), p. 225.

[21] Ibid., p. 236.

his own experience as well as from that of Dr. Gray, chief surgeon, J. J. Hospital, Bombay.

Fourth, that the factory workers earned better wages than people of the same class elsewhere. This could be proved by the Government resolution that the condition of the districts from which they came had been ameliorated by the mill industry of Bombay and that the periodical famine was not experienced as of old.

Fifth, that identical laws could be applied only to identical conditions. The application of the English factory law to Indian mills would mean ignoring the natural conditions of the country and its people. Mr. Hallett's remark related principally to the conditions of work in cotton gins and presses, where the work was sometimes hard, and where, owing to the shortness of the season and the desire of the operatives to earn enough in three or four months to keep them for the rest of the year, the hours were long. There was no parallel case of such employment in England, and it was doubtful if the English factory law would have been applied to such establishments without modification to suit the peculiar conditions of work.

Dr. Albert Leffingwell, who visited Bombay in 1881, in supporting Mr. Hallett remarked that during his observation of poverty-stricken operatives in various parts of the world, he never saw a more downhearted and apparently overworked class of working men, women, and children than that in India.[22]

Surgeon General H. Cook, M. D., F. R. C. P., who had spent 30 years in India, 15 years of which were in the City of Bombay as Principal of the Medical College and Chief of the staff of the Bombay Government Hospital, corroborated the statement of Dr. Bahadhurji in all its essential points and remarked that Mr. Hallett's paper was "greatly disfigured by exaggeration."[23] He con-

[22] International Congress of Hygiene and Demography, London, 1891. Transactions, Vol. 10, Div. 2 (Demography), p. 244.

[23] Ibid., p. 242.

tradicted the statements of Mr. Hallett and Dr. Leffingwell in their harrowing picture of Indian factory workers. "I have often passed," he said, "while driving through Bombay, crowds of operatives thronging out of the mills at dusk, and they certainly have not the exhausted and worn-out appearance depicted in Mr. Hallett's paper. They by no means look like the "driven, bullied, beaten slaves" he describes, but a throng of able-bodied operatives — laughing, singing, chatting with rapid, if not boisterous action, hastening to their homes in the enjoyment of release from labor, and the picture by no means represents a mass of wretched beings, struggling for work at any price and knowing nothing of the real pleasure of existence."[24]

Dissatisfaction in India with the New Act.

After a few months, the agitation in England for amendment of the second factory act subsided. A similar desire for the amendment also prevailed in India and was revealed by the inquiry undertaken by the India Government on behalf of the Royal Commission on Labor in Great Britain.

On January 16, 1891, the Royal Commission on Labor, appointed "to inquire into the questions affecting the relations between employers and employed, the combinations of employers and employed, and the conditions of labor,"[25] asked the Under Secretary of State for India for information on labor condition in the textile factories of India. Such information became necessary owing to "the competition of India with Lancashire in the textile trades." Following an order of the Secretary of State for India, the Government of India requested on March 14, 1892, the local governments to prepare memoranda summarising the information which the questions of the royal commission were designed to elicit. The local governments having prepared their

[24] International Congress of Hygiene and Demography, London, 1891, Transactions, Vol. 10, Div. 2 (Demography), p. 242.
[25] Gt. Brit. Parl. Papers, 1892, Vol. 34, C. 6708, p. 3.

reports, the Government of India submitted them to the Secretary of State for India on Sept. 28, 1892. "In so far as evidence was obtained with regard to the competition between India and Lancashire in the textile industries," observed the Government of India in summarising the reports, "it is stated unanimously that the condition of labor in the mills and factories is not comparable in the two countries. It is denied that India does compete with England in the spinning of finer yarns and cloth; but, even if the contrary is admitted for argument's sake, the 'loss in one branch of trade is a gain in another, in as much as the cotton spinning machinery in Indian mills is almost all imported from home'."[26]

The outstanding feature of the reports in so far as factory legislation was concerned, was a strong desire on the part of employers, employees, and philanthropists in India, to amend the recent factory act. The millowners and those who were interested in the textile trade were strongly opposed to the restrictions put by the new act on the labor of women and children. They, therefore, urged that the provisions limiting the hours of labor for women and children be repealed and that the age for the employment of boys to full time work be reduced from 14 to 12 as before. On the other hand, the employees and philanthropists did not fail to reiterate their demand for a uniform legal eleven hours' day in all factories and for provisions for compensation in case of accidents and for medical aid in case of sickness.[27]

The second factory act was, however, too new to receive any serious consideration for amendment. Like the agitation in England, these propositions did not have any practical effect on factory legislation. But the different interests voiced their opinion on the question and sooner or later they were going to force the issue into prominence.

---

[26] Gt. Brit. Parl. Papers, 1892, Vol. 36, C. 6795, p. 107—08.

[27] Ibid., p. 107.

Agitation in Scotland for regulating labor in Bengal.

Up to this time, the Manchester Chamber of Commerce in Great Britain took the most active part in the factory legislation in India. But about this time a new force appeared in the field. Like the cotton industry in Bombay, the jute industry was growing rapidly in Bengal. Jute fabrics have long formed the rough clothing of the poorer classes of people. With the invasion of cheap British cotton goods into the Indian market, jute fabrics fell into disuse and it was only with the increased exportation of grains and the consequent demand for sacks that the manufacture of gunny bags was started. The first jute factory was built at Serampore in 1854.[28] For the first few years the industry did not make any headway; then all of a sudden several factories sprang into existence and the industry began to make steady progress, as shown below:

The Growth of the Jute Industry in India.[29]

(Quinquennial averages from 1879—80 to 1893—4).

Years	number of mills	authorised capital (in lakhs of rupees)	Number in thousands of		
			Looms	spindles	persons employed
1879-80 to 1883-84	21 (100)	270.7 (100)	5.5 (100)	83 (100)	38.8 (100)
1884-5 to 1888-89	24 (114)	341.6 (126)	7 (127)	138.4 (157)	52.7 (136)
1889-90 to 1893-4	26 (124)	402.6 (149)	8.3 (151)	172.6 (196)	64.3 (166)

The above table shows that in 15 years from 1879—80 to 1893—94, the jute industry in Bengal increased 24 per cent in the number of mills, 49 per cent in the amount of capital, 51 per cent in the number of looms, 96 per cent in the number of spindles, and 66 per cent in the number of persons employed.

In the meantine a certain jute mill at Serampore, Bengal, erected electric installations and began work night and day with the help of three shifts. The progress

[28] Imperial Gazetteer of India, London, 1907, 3 : 205.
[29] Statis. of British India, Calcutta, 1921, Vol. 1, p. v.

of the jute industry and the installation of electricity for night work in Bengal aroused the spirit of rivalry of the Dundee millowners who looked upon Bengal as a source of raw jute which they would manufacture for the world market. On June 1, 1894, Sir John Leng, senior Member of Parliament for Dundee, asked the Secretary of State for India in the House of Commons whether the employment of women and young men at night in the factories in Bengal was lawful and requested him to make inquiries with a view to requiring all factories in India to conform to the rules established in the United Kingdom. In reply, the Secretary of State for India stated that it was not unlawful for factories in India to work day and night with three shifts, but women could not be employed before 5 A. M. and after 8 P. M. except with the permission of the special inspector.[30]

On the instruction of the Secretary of State for India, special inquiry was, however, started by the Government of Bengal. On September 16, 1894, after due inquiry, the Government of Bengal reported that the employment of women at night in the factory at Serampore was approved by the special inspector and was within the province of the factory law.[31]

The jute interests in Scotland were not, however, satisfied with the reply of the Bengal Government. On December 26, 1894, the Dundee Chamber of Commerce unanimously resolved to draw the attention of the Secretary of State for India to the following matters:[32]

(1) The injustice of India's competition with British textile industries, since according to the Indian factory law, women and young persons could be employed for 22 hours and children for 15 hours against 10 hours in Great Britain;

---

[30] Rept. of Committee of Bengal Chamber of Commerce, Calcutta, 1896, 1 : 1164.

[31] Ibid., pp. 1164—69.

[32] Ibid., 1896, 2 : 1163.

(2) The lack of provisions for adequate and systematic inspection by officials trained for the work as required in the United Kingdom;

(3) The evils of overwork arising from the employment of women and young persons under the provisions of the shift system.

The Chamber urged that on these grounds factories conducted by subjects of the Crown and equally under the control of Parliament, whether in India or at home, should be subjected to similar conditions.

In submitting these resolutions to the Secretary of State for India, the Chamber hoped that they would be favorably considered by the Government of India and that steps would be taken to remove the injustice complained of, and to assimilate the provisions of the Act regulating factories in India to those of the Factory Act of the United Kingdom.[33]

At the annual meeting of the Association of the Chamber of Commerce of the United Kingdom, held on March 12, 13 and 14, 1895, the resolutions passed by the Dundee Chamber of Commerce were brought forward for adoption, but were rejected. The speakers who opposed the motion pointed out the danger of intermeddling with the interests of the largest population subject to the British Crown, and contended that on grounds of imperial policy it was not wise to endeavor to force upon the possessions and colonies of the United Kingdom the same ideas of manufacture and production which were adopted in the United Kingdom. It was also pointed out that the policy which inspired the Dundee resolutions was the same policy that lost England the North American colonies. Practically on the same grounds, the Glasgow Chamber of Commerce and the Oldham Chamber of Commerce refused to support the motion of the Dundee Chamber.[34]

In the meantime, through the Government of India, the Secretary of State for India forwarded the resolutions

[33] Report of the Committee of the Bengal Chamber of Commerce, Calcutta, 1896, 1:1162.

[34] Ibid., p. 1171.

passed by the Dundee Chamber of Commerce to the Government of Bengal. On May 9, 1895, the Government of Bengal sent the resolutions to the Bengal Chamber of Commerce and to the Indian Jute Manufacturers' Association, both of which represented the cotton interests of Bengal, and asked for an expression of opinion on the matters dealt with in the resolutions and also on the necessity of amending the law regarding the employment of women and children and the adequacy of inspection.[35]

Unlike the cotton industry, the jute industry in India was controled by the British capitalists. The resolutions passed by the Dundee Chamber of Commerce created great resentment among the cotton interests. Even before the receipt of the resolutions from the Government of Bengal, the chairman of the Indian Jute Manufacturers' Association, in a speech at the annual general meeting held on March 4, 1895, strongly condemned the resolutions passed by the Dundee Chamber of Commerce. On June 28, 1895, the Association in reply to the request of the Government of Bengal sent a copy of the speech by the chairman with some additional comments. On September 24, 1895, the Bengal Chamber of Commerce also sent in their reply to the Government of Bengal. Both the Association and the Chamber strongly criticised the resolutions passed by the Dundee Chamber of Commerce and pointed out the following discrepancies:[36]

(1) All the evidence that could be gathered went to show that instead of working for 22 or even 15 hours as stated in the resolutions, women and young persons worked actually less than 8 hours a day.

(2) The inspection of factories was complete and thorough, and amply sufficient for all requirements of the Indian factory act.[37]

---

[35] Report of the Committee of the Bengal Chamber of Commerce, Calcutta, 1895, 2 : 1161.

[36] Ibid., 1895, 2 : 1170—73 & 1175—78.

[37] Ibid., 2 : 1177.

(3) Night work was then in its infancy. The natural operation of the shift system prevented overwork on the part of operatives.

Condemning the ignorance underlying the resolutions of the Dundee Chamber, the Bengal Chamber pointed out the spirit that dictated them. It was claimed that Parliament should at any cost protect Dundee and similar British industrial centres from those industries which were beyond question indigenous to India. The replies of the Bengal Chamber of Commerce and the Indian Jute Manufacturers' Association were approved of by the Government of Bengal and the Government of India.

The controversy between the jute interests in Calcutta and Dundee drew the attention of Colonel Meade King, superintending inspector of factories in Great Britain, who was special inspector of factories at Bombay in 1882. Showing the discrepancies between the factory laws in India and the United Kingdom, Colonel King maintained that some of the British manufacturers, especially in Dundee and parts of Lancashire, were severely handicapped in their competition with manufacturers in India. He claimed that factory legislation was introduced in India on the grounds of humanity and not for the purpose of protecting one class of manufacturers against another. "There is reason to believe," added Colonel King, "if we have regard to the well-being and physical improvement of our Indian fellow-subjects, that factory legislation of an earnest and thorough character is as much needed at the present moment in India as it was in Great Britain 50 years ago."[38]

Fresh Agitation in England.

In the meantime great changes were also taking place in the cotton manufacturing industry. Following the enactment of the second factory act, the industry met with one misfortune after another. For a full decade beginning with 1892, there was scarcely any year in which cotton factories worked under normal conditions. In

[38] Gt. Brit. Parl. Papers, 1896, C. 8067, 19 : 236.

1892 because of the partial failure of the crops, the price of raw cotton rose to a high point and the profits of the manufacturers were, as a consequence, materially reduced.[39] In 1893 the demonetisation of silver and the closing of the mints necessitated a readjustment of the exchange between India and the Far East, and resulted in a disturbing influence on trade. This distress was aggravated by the outbreeak of the Chino-Japanese War. The foreign exchange of India fell considerably below normal, and in 1894 the Government found itself with a deficit of about £ 2,500,000. It then became necessary to increase the revenue and in March, 1894, a tariff act was passed imposing import duties on a number of articles, but leaving cotton goods out of the schedule for fear of opposition from Manchester interests. This omission gave occasion for the rise of a strong protest even before the act was passed[40] and in the same year, it was amended, imposing a five per cent duty on cotton fabrics and yarns.

But such a procedure could scarcely be tolerated by Lancashire manufacturers without some kind of compensating measure whereby their goods could be placed on the same footing as the indigeneous products. Nor could it be sanctioned by the Secretary of State for India, especially when there were two resolutions in Parliament against such a policy. An excise duty of 5 per cent was, therefore, levied upon all cotton yarns produced in Indian factories. This amendment was followed by another amendment in 1896 by which cotton yarns were freed from taxation but a uniform duty of 3.5 per cent was imposed on all woven cotton goods, whether imported from abroad or manufactured in Indian factories.[41]

Beside these restrictions imposed by the Government upon their industry, the cotton manufacturers were confronted by other calamities. The shadow of wide-spread

---

[39] Gt. Brit. Parliamentary Papers, 1894, Vol. 58, H. of C. 108, p. 57.

[40] Gt. Brit. Parliamentary Debates, 1894, 22 : 564.

[41] Gt. Brit. Parl. Papers, 1903, Vol. 46, H. of C. 249, p. 19.

famine was cast over the country in 1896. At the same time the plague broke out in the city of Bombay and an exodus of the inhabitants, including factory laborers, practically stopped the operation of the factories. The depression of the previous years soon reached a crisis culminating in 1900—01, when the price of coal went up. The succession of these distressing events led to the closing of 16 factories during the year. A large number of others worked only half time. The output of certain yarns dropped from 514,000,000 lbs. in 1899—1900 to 353,000,000 lbs. in 1900—1901.[42]

But, in spite of these adverse conditions, the cotton industry did not cease making progress. During the decade from 1891—92 to 1900—01, the number of factories rose from 127 to 190, the number of looms from 24,670 to 40,542 and of spindles from 3,268,524 to 4,932,602. At the same time, the amount of capital invested in cotton industries rose from £ 7,844,000 to £ 11,170,000 as shown in the table below.

Growth of the Cotton Industry from 1891—92 to 1900—01.

	1891-92[43]	1900-01
Factories	127	190
Looms	24,670	40,542
Spindles	3,268,524	4,932,602
Capital	£ 7,844,000	£ 11,170,000

In brief, since the last year of the previous decennial period, the number of factories increased by 49 per cent, of looms and of spindles by 64.3 and 50.9 per cent respectively, and the amount of capital by 42.4 per cent.[44]

[42] Gt. Brit. Parl. Papers, 1903, Vol. 46, H. of C. 249, pp. 228—29.

[43] The slight discrepancies in the figures for 1890—91 in this and the other table on page 39 are due to different sources of information which include or exclude some of the native states.

[44] Gt. Brit. Parl. Papers, 1903, Vol. 46, H. of C. 249, p. 229.

In 1901—02 the cotton crop was comparatively large and the consequent cheaper price of raw cotton led to the partial resumption of activity by the factories. This temporary activity was soon followed by another depression, and in 1903—04 several mills ceased from operating or worked for part time. But the year 1904—05 saw a complete revolution in the cotton industry of India. A large crop again cheapened the price of raw cotton and at the same time a profitable market was opened both at home and abroad. The factories resumed their work with full force and a state of unusual activity followed. From 1900—01 to 1904—05, the outturn of yarn rose from 342,777,500 to 555,948,400 lbs. and of woven goods from 95,844,600 to 152,741,800 lbs.[45]

This sudden boom, especially after so many years of depression led to such activity as could scarcely be confined to the normal working conditions. Although all the spindles were brought into operation, the factories could not meet the demand of the market. Overwork soon resulted. The factories, fitted with electric light, prolonged the hours of work much beyond the usual time.

The *Times of India*, an Anglo-Indian journal at Bombay, started a strong agitation against this overwork. Column after column of the paper was filled with the description of abuses in the Bombay factories. The *Pioneer*, another Anglo-Indian journal at Allahabad, also published several articles strongly protesting against this overtime work. Though much of what the Anglo-Indian press said was exaggerated, the existence of long hours of work could not be denied even by employers themselves. The Bombay Millowner's Association went so far as to pass a resolution limiting the hours of work in their factories. But it could not be enforced in a time of such unusual industrial activity without state authority.[46]

The agitation of the *Times of India* and other papers drew the attention of the Government to the matter of long hours, and an inquiry was started by the

---

[45] Gt. Brit. Parl. Papers, 1907, Vol. 59, H. of C. 149, pp. 176—177.

[46] *Ibid.*, 1908, Vol. 74, Cd. 4292, p. 7.

collector of Bombay. The collector informed the Government of Bombay on June 24, 1905, that out of 74 mills, the exact working hours of which had been ascertained, 16 mills worked 14 hours or more a day and 33 worked 13 hours or more.[47]

About this time a momentous event took place in the Indian national life. The Government of India conceived the idea of the partition of Bengal. This province, the people of which spoke the same language, was to be divided and joined to other provinces inhabited by peoples speaking different languages. The proposed partition created a feeling of deep indignation among the Bengalees. They appealed to the Government, but without success. In their desperation, they boycotted all British goods by a resolution on August 7, 1905. And this boycott was soon turned into Swadeshi, or movement for the use of country-made goods.

Bengal was partitioned on October 16, 1905. The Bengalees observed the date as the day of mourning. The boycott movement spread rapidly. Meeting after meeting was held all over the province, renewing the vow. Small indigenous industries began to spring up in different parts of the country. The handloom industry was revived and the leaders of the movement even started a new cotton factory in Bengal. Some of the cotton factories in other provinces turned their attention to catering to the needs of the Bengalees, who had so long been supplied with goods by Lancashire manufacturers.

The actual loss of the British trade due do to the boycott was rather small and temporary. But considerable apprehension was neverthless felt by Manchester interests at the resolution of the Bengalees, who bought more than half of the goods they exported into India. On the other hand, unusual activity in Indian cotton factories again created the spirit of rivalry among them. They had repealed the import duty, or at least compelled the Indian Government to levy an excise duty in order to counterbalance it. Restriction had already been put on

[47] Gt. Brit. Parl. Papers, 1908, Vol. 74, Cd. 4292, p. 7.

child and woman labor in Indian factories. But adult male labor was still unrestricted and it was this phase of Indian factory labor to which they now devoted their energy.

On March 14, 1906, a deputation from the United Textile Factory Workers' Association of Lancashire waited upon Mr. John Morley, then Secretary of State for India, regarding the conditions of work in Indian factories. By means of quotations from the Bombay *Times of India*, the deputation called attention of the Secretary of State to the long hours of work in Bombay factories, and asked for a more effective system of factory inspection, and urged the necessity of reducing the working hours of all factory laborers by legislative measures. It was not a question of competition, but simply one of humanity, observed the deputation. In reply, Mr. Morley pointed out that the present delegation did not represent the Lancashire point of view, that it would be a misfortune were it to get abroad that any action which the Government might take in the matter was in the least due to the pressure from Lancashire, and that the thing which ought to be kept in mind was not competition or convenience of employers, but the welfare of the employees. Regarding the long hours of work, Mr. Morley said that the Government of India had the question fully brought to its notice. The reports of the newspapers were not fully reliable, but the cases of excessive hours of work were known to have existed in Bombay factories. The latest report of the chief inspector of factories showed, however, that these hours had been voluntarily reduced from 15 to 13. As to the inspection of factories, Mr. Morley replied that the Government of India realized the necessity of increasing the number of inspectors; perhaps a more efficient and elaborate system of factory inspection was desirable.

As far as the reduction of the working hours of adult males by legislation was concerned, the Government of India did not think that the necessity of having recourse to such a method had been established. Legislative restriction on the working hours of adult males would mean the introduction of a new principle in factory legislation, which Mr. Morley said, was a burning question in Great Britain itself and would perhaps be more difficult in India. He admitted, however, that Indian employees had no representative and self-chosen authority to speak for them and, therefore, depended entirely upon the vigilant, effective and constant supervision by the supreme authority of all relations of employers to the Factory Act of 1891. After assuring the deputation that it would not be difficult to impress the Government of India with the necessity of using its best offices in this matter, he promised to send out an English factory inspector to investigate the actual conditions in Indian factores.[48]

Sir H. P. Frier-Smith, a former superintending inspector for dangerous trades in England, was soon appointed for this duty.

Textile Factory Labor Committee of 1906.

On the advice of the Secretary of State for India, the Government of India appointed, on December 17, 1906, a small committee to inquire into the conditions of labor in textile factories. The committee consisted of three members, of whom Sir H. P. Frier-Smith, R. N., was president.

The specific points upon which the committee was instructed to report, were the following:[49]

(1) Whether the working hours of adult males should be limited and whether the physique of operatives was affected by long hours.

(2) Whether certificates of age and physical fitness of children should be required before they were allowed to work in factories.

(3) Whether the minimum age of children should be raised beyond 9.

(4) Whether, as the result of employment as adults of persons between the ages of 12 and 14, there had been

---

[48] The T i m e s, London, March 15, 1906, p. 15, c. 5.
[49] Gt. Brit. Parl. Papers, 1907, Vol. 59, Cd. 3617, p. 5.

physical deterioration requiring the creation by law of a special class of workers to be known as young persons.

(5) Whether a separate staff of medical factory inspectors should be provided for.

(6) Whether dangerous machinery should be more adequately fenced.[50]

The committee met at Bombay on December 21, 1906, and visited Ahmedabad, Calcutta, Madras, Delhi, Agra, Cawnpore and Nagpore. They inspected 121 factories and several workingmen's *chawls* or dwellings, and examined a large number of witnesses comprising employers and employees, special and medical inspectors of factories and others. The results of their investigation were submitted on April 5, 1907. The recommendations were based firstly on the British factory act of 1901, and embodied the following:

(1) That the hours of work for adult males should be regulated. The Indian laborer could, of course, stand higher temperature than the British workman, and the temperature in the best mills was not of a kind to cause ill-health or serious discomfort. But the committee found that the introduction of electric light had led to longer hours of work and in busy seasons there was a tendency to overwork. Employers had themselves realized the necessity of regulating the hours, but had not been successful in coming to a common understanding among themselves. Employees were desirous of shorter hours and had also made petition to the government to that effect. The committee was of the opinion that trade would not suffer from such restrictions.[51]

The period of employment in factories, except for those working on the shift system, should be fixed between the hours of either 5.30 A. M. or 6 A. M. and 6.30 P. M. The engine should stop for half an hour between the hours of 12 noon and 2 P. M. In mills working on the shift system, the period of employment should, as at present,

---

[50] This question was added later on. Gt. Brit. Parl. Papers, 1907, Vol. 59, Cd. 3617, p. 6.

[51] *Ibid.*, p. 15—17.

be between 5 A. M. and 8 P. M., provided that the actual period of employment for adult males should never exceed 12 hours in any one day.[52]

Regarding the physique of operatives, the committee could not get any definite information other than that given by the Medical Committee of 1884.

(2) That the night work of women should be altogether prohibited. The night emnloyment of women in textile factories was exceptional. But in seasonal employments, such as cotton gins, it was rather common. There were two possible evil effects of such a system: — First, the women had to take their children with them to the place of work, where the atmosphere, especially at night under artificial light, was unpleasant and not conducive to health, or they had to leave them at home, generally speaking, uncared for. Second, they frequently worked at household duties in the day time after working a whole night in a gin. It had often been argued that seasonal employments did not last more than three to five months and that delay in manipulation of cotton might lead to serious loss. In reply the committee said that boys over fourteen could be employed as adults, and if arrangements were gradually made, the inconvenience might be greatly lessened, if not entirely removed.[53]

(3) That there should not be any young person class, but the names of all persons under the age of 16 should be entered in a prescribed register. Classification of employees on the basis of age was very hard and the creation of such a class would cause serious difficulty in administration. Even under the existing law, a large number of workers were employed as adults long before they had attained the age of 14. But such abuses could be avoided, the committee argued, by a physical examination prior to employment on full time.[54]

(4) That certificate of age and physical fitness should be required of all children prior to both half-time and full-

[52] Gt. Brit. Parl. Papers, 1907, Vol. 59, Cd. 3617, p. 17.
[53] Ibid., p. 15.
[54] Ibid., pp. 19—20.

time employment. The certificate should be personal property of the child to whom it applied, and be carried by him while at work.[55] The committee also recommended that the minimum age of 9 for the employment of children was sufficient and should not be raised. There were no facilities for school attendance throughout the country and many of these children would, therefore, be employed in places not under the factory act, where the conditions of work might be worse or more exausting, or, if unemployed, they would possibly be idling in the bazaars instead of honestly earning a small sum towards family expenses. Clear and definite laws should be made requiring the employment of half time children only in sets, either in the morning or in the afternoon, or in the double set system so common in Indian factories. Efficient measures should be taken to see that children should work only in proper sets and that the prescribed hours of labor were not exceeded.[56]

(5) That dry bulb thermometers should be placed in all humid cotton factories, readings should be taken at fixed times and the returns forwarded monthly. These returns should be eventually considered with a view to regulating the amount of moisture necessary for manufacturing processes to the health of employees.[57]

The other recommendations regarding sanitation dealt with the fixation of a purity standard for the water used in introducing moisture into mills, the registration of the date of lime washing, and the provision of adequate latrine accommodation. As regards safety, the committee recommended the opening of factory doors from the inside and a more elaborate system of fencing dangerous machinery.[58]

(6) Furthermore the committee recommended that arrangement should be made to secure uniformity of administration of the factory act throughout the country,

---

[55] Gt. Brit. Parl. Papers, 1907, Vol. 59, Cd. 3617, p. 11.
[56] Ibid., p. 14.
[57] Ibid., pp. 22—23.
[58] Ibid., pp. 23—28.

that the system of inspection and the strength and composition of the staff of inspectors should be considered with a view to securing efficiency, and that full-time medical inspectors should be appointed. Inefficiently administered, the law might do more harm than good. Employers were apt to think that when there was state inspection, they were relieved of their responsibility. A number of medical officers, the committee believed, should be assigned to each separate area and, subject to the department of commerce and industry, they should be the supreme authority on all medical matters relating to labor. Special inspectors should not be relieved of the duties relative to sanitary matters, but they should take instructions from medical inspectors on all such points and refer to them all doubtful cases.[59]

Factory Labor Commission of 1907.

The textile factory labor committee was appointed to make only a preliminary investigation and it was promised that should the report of the committee establish the existence of alleged abuses, which required remedying, a comprehensive investigation would be undertaken by a representative commission before any radical change in the existing factory law. The committee reporting on the necessity of several alterations in the existing law, the Government of India, with the approval of the Secretary of State, appointed, on October 10, 1907,

[59] Gt. Brit. Parl. Papers, 1907, Vol. 59, Cd. 3617, pp. 8—10.

[60] Ibid., 1908, Vol. 74, Cd. 4292, pp. 1—2.

The following gentlemen were the members of the commission: — Mr. W. A. B. Beaumont, superintending inspector of factories, England; Mr. S. M. Chitnavis, B. A., I. C. S., deputy commissioner, Central Provinces; Lieut. Col. C. MacTaggart, M. A., inspector-general of prisons, United Provinces; The Hon. Mr. Alexander McRobert, representative of the Upper India Chamber of Commerce; Dr. T. M. Nair, municipal commissioner, Madras; Mr. John Nicoll, representative of the Bengal Chamber of Commerce; and the Hon. Mr. Vithaldas Damodher Thackersey, representative of the Bombay Chamber of Commerce and the Bombay Mill-Owners' Association. Mr. J. Campbell, I. C. S., undersecretary to the Government of India, department of commerce and industry, served as secretary.

a commission[60] with the Hon. Mr. W. T. Morrison, I. C. S., officiating member of the Council of Bombay, as president.

The members of the commission assembled at Bombay on November 1, 1907, and visited 209 factories of all descriptions located at Bombay and 23 other industrial centers. They also sent out questionnaires to various groups of people, such as (a) employers, agents, and managers of factories, gins, and presses; (b) representatives of various local governments; (c) medical practitioners and other persons who might in any way be interested in factory legislation. The written evidence of about 275 witnesses was supplemented by oral examination. The interests of employers were well represented by 8 chambers of commerce and 4 millowners' associations. As employees did not have any organization and as they were afraid of incurring the displeasure of their employers by openly giving evidence, the president of the commission and one of the members visited the dwellings of several employees at Bombay, Ahmedabad, Delhi, Cawnpore and Calcutta. The report of the commission was submitted in May, 1908. Mr. Vithaldas Damodher Thackersey, one of the members of the commission, signed his name with the reservation of a minute of dissent. But Dr. Nair, another member, could not agree with the majority of the commission on several important points, and made, therefore, a separate report.

Like the Textile Factory Labor Committee, the commission also based its recommendations on the British factory and workshop act of 1901. (1) The most important recommendation of the commission was that the working hours of adult males should be limited to 12 hours a day, but no direct restrictive measure should be adopted for the attainment of such an object. Regarding the necessity of such a limitation, the commission fully agreed with the committee. With the exception of cotton and jute mills and the weaving departments of silk mills, excessive hours, i. e., hours over 12 a day were not worked in Indian factories. In factories working daylight hours, the average working day for the whole year was approximately 12 hours and 5 minutes. But the longest work day in summer was 13½ hours and the shortest in winter, 11 hours. In the Bombay mills fitted with electric light, the hours varied from 13 to 13½ a day. In the latter part of 1905 the Bombay mills worked even 14½ hours a day, though only for a short time. Long hours of work were prevalent in some parts of Northern India. Under these circumstances, the limitation of working hours had become necessary. The Bombay employers realised the importance of this limitation in 1905, but were unable to enforce it.

On the other hand, there was a considerable number of employees who would like to work longer hours, if they could earn correspondingly higher wages thereby. Though no direct proof had hitherto been found to show that long hours of work affected the physique of employees injuriously, yet the continuance of this practice could not but lead to such a consequence. Moreover, long hours of work would tend to make factory labor unpopular in India and, therefore, the development of the industry would suffer. The majority of employees wished to have their hours regulated, because they were not yet able to combine over any large area with the object of securing a common end by concerted action. It was, therefore, the duty of the Government to prevent the recurrence, or continuation, of such practices on both economic and humanitarian grounds. But the commission could not support the recommendation of the committee for direct restrictions on adult male labor for the following reasons:[61]

First, that no case had been made out in favor of applying a principle which was admittedly of doubtful validity, which commanded acceptance in a very few countries, and which supplied a remedy very much more drastic than the circumstances of the case demanded.

Second, the direct limitation of the working hours of adult males would impose on all classes of factories a restriction which was found to require only in the case of textile factories.

---

[61] Gt. Brit. Parl. Papers, 1908, Vol. 84, Cd. 4292, pp. 31—33.

Third, the enforcement of any law rigidly restricting the working hours of adult males was strongly objected to in India. In all industries overtime was frequently necessary. It was not possible to devise any workable system of exceptions which would give employers the freedom they could legitimately claim, and at the same time secure the general enforcement of the restrictions. The direct restrictions of the hours of work for adult males existed in France, where the law provided numerous exceptions. There were 91 factory inspectors in France and the notice of availing oneself of these exceptions could be given to any of them. But such a system would be utterly unworkable in India, beeause the area over which the factories were scattered was vast, the number of inspectors small, and the employers in smaller factories were very imperfectly educated. Moreover, no exceptions could be made in advance for new industries which were springing up and which it was necessary to foster and encourage in every possible way. Official procedure always involved considerable delay.

Fourth, a direct restriction on the hours of adult labor would be repugnant to the great majority of capitalists, both Indian and European, who had already invested or were thinking of investing money. This was clear from the evidence given by a large number of witnesses. Such a measure would, therefore, check further investment and consequently hamper the growth of industry.

Fifth, there was reason to fear that, if legislation was undertaken to limit the working hours of adults to 12 or 13 hours, it would not stop there and attempts would be made in the future — not always suggested merely by the idea of doing justice to the operatives — to restrict still further their working hours.

"We are strongly opposed", concluded the commission, "to any direct limitation of adults' working hours, because we consider that there is no necessity for the adoption of this drastic course, because we are convinced that it would cause the greatest inconvenience to existing industries, most of which have never worked long hours, and because we think that such a measure would seriously hamper the growth of industrial enterprise".[62]

The commission, therefore, recommended the following measures for an indirect limitation of working hours:[63]

(a) Formation of a young person class comprising all young persons between the ages of 14 and 17, with working hours limited to 12 in any one day.

(b) Reduction of the working hours of children from 7 to 6.

(c) Prohibition of the employment of "young persons", women and children before 5.30 A. M. or after 7 P. M.

(d) Substitution of a compulsory interval of rest after six hours' continuous work in place of a present midday interval.

(e) Assimilation of the restrictions placed upon the employment of women into those proposed for the "young person" class.

The commission was fully convinced that the hours of rest fixed for children and "young persons" would absolutely determine the working hours of all persons employed in cotton spinning. The work of doffing could not be quickly and expertly done by men. Neither were male adults good piecers, for in this work nimbleness of fingers and smallness of stature were essential. It was safe to assume that about one-third of the staff in the spinning department would be composed of young persons between 14 and 17 years of age. The number of the protected class (women and children) in the weaving department was not so large that their hours would determine the working hours of the whole department. But the machinery in the spinning and the weaving departments was in almost all cases driven by the same engine. It would not be economical to run one department while the other remained idle. Moreover, the weavers in cotton mills, because of the higher wages they earned, were much more independent than the spinners. They had, in many cases,

---

[62] Gt. Brit. Parl. Papers, 1909, Vol. 63, Cd. 4519, p. 185.
[63] Ibid., 1908, Vol. 74, Cd. 4292, p. 33.

refused to work the same number of hours as the spinners, and could not possibly be induced to work longer hours.

There was scarcely any possibility of working male adults for 12½ hours, i. e., from 5.30 A. M. to 7 P. M. with the shift system arranged for the protected class. The shift system in such a case would not be possible. Nor would it be profitable to resume work for half an hour after stopping work at the end of every sixth hour, which would be required by the measure proposed.

The fact that they were relieved of the necessity of having "young persons" registered or certified of age before their employment in the new capacity, would be a strong inducement to employers to adopt a 12 hour day. A 12 hour day would also give an opportunity to women and children to go to the factory in the morning with their male relatives, and all the members of a family except the children on the morning shift could return home together in the evening. The enforcement of a 12 hour day for children and "young persons" would further create a feeling for a 12 hour day all over the country. A large number of employers in Bombay had already been anxious to follow a 12 hour day.

Dr. Nair dissented from the majority of his colleagues and recommended a direct legislative restriction of adult male labor. The chief points upon which he took issue were: First, that almost all the workers in the weaving department were adult males. The regulation of the working hours of women, "young persons" and children would not, therefore, protect the weavers. The weaving department might be worked with separate machinery, e. g., in the Empress Mill at Nagpur, or it might be worked longer than the spinning department, e. g., in Bengal cotton mills, or the work of the proposed young person class might be altogether dispensed with. Second, employees were practically unanimous in asking for a legislative restriction of their hours of labor. Employers themselves were also desirous of achieving the same end. Dr. Nair's minute of dissent did not arrive in time to be commented upon by the commission.[64]

[64] Gt. Brit. Parl. Papers, 1908, Vol. 74, Cd. 4292, pp. 81—104.

Mr. Vithaldas D. Thackersey contended in his minute of dissent that factories having no arrangement for electric light might be allowed to work daylight hours.[65] But the commission rejected the suggestion on several grounds: — First, it would raise the working hours in Northern India to 13½ hours of actual work during the hottest period of the year. Second, it would deprive employees of the enjoyment of a single hour of daylight at their home. Third, it would necessitate the working of children and "young persons" for more than 6 and 12 hours respectively. Fourth, it would prevent all improvement in the habit and efficiency of employees. The hot weather days were so long and the climatic and other conditions were so trying that employees naturally dawdled over their work as much as possible. Fifth, it would make possible for many of the employees to work long hours during the hot weather by daylight and then accept employment in cold weather in mills working a fixed 12 hours by electric light, as a considerable number of employees were willing to earn higher wages by working excessive hours. Sixth, it would be impossible to work two systems side by side in the same place.[66]

(2) The commission recommended allowing women to work the same number of hours as the young person class, i. e., 12 hours a day. The general physical condition of woman workers in various parts of the country visited by the commission was uniformly excellent. The women at Pondichery, where the French Government allowed them to work 12 hours a day throughout the year, were found by two members of the commission "a robust and healthy lot". This finding was also substantiated by the evidence of the medical witnesses examined by the commission as well as by the result of inspection conducted by Lieutenant Colonel MacTaggart throughout the Bombay Presidency. For these reasons the commission was satisfied that women could work 12 hours a day without danger to their health. The interval of rest for an hour and a half, as prescribed by the ex-

[65] Gt. Brit. Parl. Papers, 1908, Vol. 74, Cd. 4292, pp. 75—76.
[66] Ibid., pp. 56—57.

isting law in case of a full day's work, was found in practice to be too long. It was essential to the success of the proposal of the commission that the hours of work and the interval of rest for both women and young persons should be identical in all respects. There would be several advantages from such a measure: — First, a new avenue of employment would be opened to women and they would thus be able to recover the position which they had held prior to the introduction of the existing restrictions on their hours of work. The benefit of it had been perceived even by the Factory Commission of 1890. Second, it would help to relieve the scarcity of labor in textile factories. Third, it would also bind down employers of labor more closely to the acceptance of a general 12 hour day in factories.[67]

Here again, Dr. Nair objected to the proposal of the commission that the working time of women should be increased.[68]

(3) The commission proposed that all workers between the ages of 14 and 17 should be included within the young person class and that their actual working hours should be limited to 12 in any one day.[69]

Hon. Vithaldas Damodher Thackersey differed from the rest of his colleagues and proposed 12½ hours' work for the proposed young persons and 6¼ hours' work for children. The decision of the commission was based on the observation of thousands of persons of the ages between 14 and 17 and on the minute inspection of 2000 of them. As such young persons were likely to suffer permanently from overwork and as they, owing to immaturity of judgment, were prone to overwork, their work should be regulated by law.

The Factory Commission of 1890 was opposed to the creation of a young person class between half-timers and full-timers on the ground that the members of such a class would be squeezed out of employment in factories, since their working hours could be fitted to that of neither

[67] Gt. Brit. Parl. Papers, 1908, Vol. 74, Cd. 4292, pp. 45—46.
[68] Ibid., pp. 104—105.
[69] Ibid., pp. 40—42.

half-timers nor full-timers. That commission had also considered it unnecessary to impose any restrictions on the labor of persons over 14, as at that age many of them assumed the responsibility of a family. But the proposal of a 12 hour day by law eliminated the danger of this class being squeezed out, or forced to work as half-timers, for young persons under the proposed regulation would work the same hours as adult males and double the hours of children. Moreover, it was not borne out by facts that Indian children married or were about to be married at the age of 14.[70]

The Textile Factory Labor Committee of 1906 objected to the creation of a young person class on the ground that it would create serious administrative inconvenience in actual working. But this objection would be met by the proposal that all factories, which undertook to work a 12 hour day, would be exempted from the necessity of having their young persons registered, or certified of age. The half-timers would be permitted to enter the young person class without further medical examination, when the medical certificate, obtained by them prior to admission as half-timers, showed that they had reached the age of 14. Physical examination in such cases would also be eliminated. The physique of this class was, on the whole, very satisfactory. Out of a thousand young persons, specially selected for recommendation, less than 2.5 per cent were considered physically unfit, apart from the age requirement. A large number of witnesses was opposed to the creation of such a class on the ground of administrative difficulty. But when the above method of administration was explained to them, the opposition was at once withdrawn.[71]

(4) The commission recommended that children over 9 and under 14 years of age should not be allowed to work more than six hours in any one day. The strain of the present working hours had affected children more severely than any other class of workers. To increase the minimum

[70] Gt. Brit. Parl. Papers, 1908, Vol. 74, Cd. 4292, pp. 41—42.
[71] Ibid., pp. 41—43.

age would not solve the problem, for parents might send them to some other work of a more exhaustive nature, as the committee had already suggested. Children should be employed either continuously for 6 hours, or in broken periods not exceeding 6 hours in all, provided always that the total period of employment was comprised within 8½ consecutive hours. The commission found the employment of children under 9 to be one of the most serious abuses in factories and endorsed the recommendation of the committee regarding the certifying of age and physical fitness prior to employment.[72]

(5) As to the time for beginning and closing work, the commission proposed that women, young persons, and children should not be allowed to work except between the hours of 5.30 A. M. and 7 P. M., local mean time.[73] Under the existing law women and children were allowed to work between the hours of 5 A. M. and 8 P. M. In many factories, e. g., those in Bengal, the work began at 5 A. M. and, as the children had to walk from two to three miles before arriving at the factory, they were obliged to get up long before the daybreak, a condition regarded as one of the causes of the shortage of child labor. Women often worked late; they could not go home in the darkness and had to wait until some other worker, a relative or husband, accompanied them. And a period of absence from home of one or two hours longer than the actual hours spent in the factory work resulted in a condition that was not only detrimental to health, but also interfered with household duties. This time limitation could naturally not be applied to seasonal employments, where the conditions were different.

(6) The commission recommended that seasonal occupations should be brought under the provision of the act, whether they worked for more than four months or not. Women and young persons should be permitted to work in gins at night. But their work should not exceed more than 12 hours a day. It might be considered a

---

[72] Gt. Brit. Parl. Papers, 1908, Vol. 74, Cd. 4292, pp. 43—45.
[73] Ibid., p. 47.

sufficient compliance with the law, if additional workers were employed to the extent necessary to reduce the hours of work of each woman and young person to not more than 12 hours, assuming that the work, during the total period for which the gin ran, was uniformly distributed among all workers.[74]

(7) The question of safety and sanitation was also considered and the commission made various recommendations on the line laid down by the committee. The commission did not, however, think that any standard of humidity could be fixed for a vast country like India, which had a variety of climate.[75] But provisions should be made for protecting workers from inhaling dust or other impurities. Machinery was, in most cases, well fenced, but fire escapes should be provided for those who worked in the upper stories of a factory building.

(8) The commission did not favor compelling factory owners to provide elementary education for children in their employment, as there was no analogous provision in India which could be cited in support of the proposal. Special schools for factory children could, however, be opened at suitable centres close to factories. These schools should be financed by local authorities assisted by factory owners. Children should be allowed to attend school only two hours a day. To encourage education, the age limit for inclusion in the class of young persons might be reduced by one year, if a child was physically fit and passed an educational test.

(9) The commission concluded that the present system of inspection had failed on account of the inadequacy of the staff and of the custom of appointing ex-officio inspectors. It recommended the appointment of whole time inspectors, but did not approve of the proposal of the committee for the appointment of separate medical inspectors.[77] Previous experience in factory work in England was not considered necessary for eligibility, although

---

[74] Gt. Brit. Parl. Papers, 1908, Vol. 74, Cd. 4292, p. 53.
[75] Ibid., pp. 61—63.
[76] Ibid., p. 59.
[77] Ibid., p. 69.

inspectors without such experience might, on appointment, be placed for three months with a factory inspector in the United Kingdom. Experience in India, on the other hand, and a knowledge of the vernacular of the province in which an inspector was employed, were considered highly desirable.[78]

The reports of the committee and the commission gave rise to comments and discussion both in India and in England. The proposal of the committee recommending the direct restriction of adult laborers was strongly protested against in India. The Indian newspapers and also a section of the Anglo-Indian press raised their voice against such a novel measure in Indian legislation and one which had been avoided by British legislation. The recommendations of the commission even for the indirect limitation of adult male labor to 12 hours per day and of child labor to 6 hours, were also strongly criticised. The Indian Jute Mills' Association of Calcutta addressed the Government, on September 16, 1908, stating that 90 per cent of the jute mill industry in Bengal was opposed to any alteration or amendment of the existing factory law. "It is more effective administration," asserted the Association, "of the existing law that is required rather than fresh legislation".[79]

The soundness of the principle of a 12 hour day for the improvement of the general health and conditions of life of the laboring classes was seriously doubted by the Upper India Chamber of Commerce. The chamber contended that strenuous work was foreign to the habit and inclination of Asiatic laborers and to the conditions of the climate of the country and the temperament of the people. Under the 12 hour system, both the employer and the worker would experience a new compulsion for strenuous work; the former from the necessity which he would be under of obtaining the output essential to profitable working; the latter from the additional effort which he must put forth to earn the wages which he had earned under exist-

---

[78] Gt. Brit. Parl. Papers, 1908, Vol. 74, Cd. 4292, p. 69.

[79] Bengal Chamber of Commerce Report, 1908, Calcutta, Vol. 2, pp. 588—89.

ing conditions. The chamber regarded with serious misgivings the consequences likely to result from arousing discontent among all those engaged in industrial enterprise, whether employers or employees.[80]

Introduction of the Bill into the Legislature.

On July 30, 1909, Mr. W. L. Harvey made the motion in the Legislative Council of India to withdraw the bill introduced on September 29, 1905, to amend the factory act and also to introduce a new bill to amend and consolidate the Indian factory law. The main proposal made in the new bill was "to regulate by law the hours of work of all factory operatives in the largest and most important class of factories".[81] Referring to the statement of Lord Lansdowne that the Factory Act of 1891 would be accepted, both in India and in England, "as a settlement as final as any settlement of such a question" could be, Mr. Harvey pointed out that the conditions under which such a statement was made had altogether changed through the installment of electric light in factories, especially those of Bombay. The new conditions had placed before both employers and employees the temptation to exceed inordinately the regular hours of work, which were formerley 12 on the average for the year, whenever an opportunity occurred. The possibility of such abuses was clearly shown by the prosperity of the year 1904—05, when the daily hours of work rose to 15 in some cases.

The Government was, therefore, bound to reopen the question of factory legislation. The Textile Factory Labor Committee of 1906 and the Factory Labor Commission of 1907, both appointed by the Government for investigation and recommendation on the matter, had advised further regulation of factories, the former recommending direct intervention to limit the hours of adult male labor. Moreover, all local governments, except the Government of Burma, were in favor of further legislative interferences.

---

[80] India, Legislative Council Proceedings, Calcutta, 1910—11, 49 : 584.

[81] Ibid., 1909—10, 48 : 1.

Several commercial bodies held the same views, though one or two chambers of commerce and certain trade associations, representing factory owners, were opposed to any such proposal. The necessity of further legislation being established, the question arose whether the restriction on the working hours of adult male labor should be direct or indirect. The Government had decided in favor of direct restriction. The commission was opposed to such a direct measure on the grounds that it would cause great inconvenience to the existing industries and seriously hamper the growth of industrial enterprise and that the same result could be achieved by the creation of a young person class with their hours of work limited to 12 a day. The Government raised three issues to the objections of the commission: —

First, are the objections to direct restriction as serious as the commission supposed them to be? The commission questioned the validity of direct regulation on the ground of principle and pointed out the necessity for restriction at the same time. But the necessity of Government intervention being conceded, the question did not involve any new principle except expediency and administrative convenience. The contention that such a procedure had found acceptance in only a few countries overlooked the fact that labor in India was not organised. To meet the objection that only one class of factories worked excessive hours and that the law, if enacted, would apply to all cases, the Government proposed to legislate for that class only and reserved the power at the same time to extend the provision of the law to other classes, should the necessity to do so arise. Another objection raised by the commission was that overtime was frequently required in all industries and that in India it would be impossible to devise a workable system of exceptions, which would give employers the freedom they could legitimately claim and would at the same time secure the general enforcement of the restrictions. But it would not be hard to devise a workable system of exceptions. Moreover, the members of the commission themselves did not escape the difficulty by resort to indirect method.

They proposed that all factories which undertook to work for not more than 12 hours a day, should be exempted from the necessity of having their "young persons" registered and certified of age. But it was obvious, Mr. Harvey said, that if a large number of factories accepted this alternative, the position would at once be the same, as if the 12 hour day had been imposed by law, and the task of working out a system of exceptions would still have to be undertaken by the Government.

Second, would the 12 hour day for the proposed young person class between 14 and 17 automatically limit the hours of work for adult males also? The commission recommended, in this connection, raising the working hours of women to 12 and reducing at the same time the working hours of children to 6. The creation of a young person class would increase administrative difficulties; for it would be hard, as the committee had pointed out, to determine the age. The increase in the working hours of women would be a retrograte step. It had not been shown that women could work regularly 12 hours a day without detriment to their health, nor that it was desirable that they should compete with men for the same kind of work to a larger extent than they did.

Third, would the indirect method prove successful? There were three possible methods of frustating the object in view. In the first place, factories might do away with the services of women and young persons altogether. In the second place, if, owing to scarcity of labor, all the factories did not dispense with the employment of women and of young persons, some of them at least might take that course. In such cases, the existence side by side of factories working both restricted and unrestricted hours would create an unfortunate situation. In the third place, women and "young persons" in a factory might be segregated in certain departments where a 12 hour rule might be observed; while in the rest of the factory the unrestricted long hours of work might still be continued. Factories might even be established for weaving only, where the services of women and young persons would scarcely be utilised.

With these difficulties in mind, the Government could not follow the recommendations of the commission and had to propose direct regulation of the hours of adult male labor. The provisions of the proposed bill were divided into two classes: — First, those which applied to non-textile factories. The only changes in connection with them were a compulsory midday stoppage for rest, and a weekly holiday. Second, those which applied to textile factories. The changes in connection with them were that the work of all male operatives should be limited to 12 hours in any one day, thus avoiding the necessity of creating a young person class and of increasing the hours of women, and that women and children should not be employed in any factory before 5.30 A. M. and after 7 P. M., unless there was an approved shift system in force. Special exceptions were to be proposed by the Government for the employment of women and children in seasonal employments.

The bill also contained a provision for the certification of the age and physical condition of children before they could actually be employed in a factory. It was also provided that when a child over six years of age was found in a factory, it should be presumed that he was actually employed until the contrary was proved. The other provisions of the bill related to sanitation, responsibility for infringement of the law, etc. The bill was introduced on the same day; a draft was, as usual, sent to the local governments, but it was not until 1911 that it was again taken up in the legislative council.

Reference of the Bill to the Select Committee.

On January 3, 1911, Hon. B. Robertson made the motion that the bill for the consolidation and amendment of the law regulating labor in factories should be referred to a select committee and stated that since the introduction of the bill, nothing had happened to change the decision of the Government on the important provision for regulating adult male labor in cotton factories.

Before the motion was carried, the bill was strongly protested by several members of the council, who were opposed to further restrictions on factory labor, especially to that on adult male labor. First, the bill was shown to be of "ignoble origin". It was argued that the unfortunate anxiety of the Government for the protection of Lancashire manufacturers determined and colored the policy of the bill. Rao Bahadur R. N. Mudholkar, representing the interests of seasonal establishments, pointed out that the boom in Indian textile industries in 1904—06 aroused the fear of those who were interested in importation into India of an ever-increasing quantity of textiles. It was they who raised the cry of overwork in Indian factories and it was their agitation that resulted in the appointment of a commission for the framing of the bill. "The bill", continued the Rao Bahadur, "is not one which was brought forward by the Government of India of its own accord, or suggested by any local government. It was not demanded by the laborers; it was not demanded by any of the interests concerned in the country. It came from persons who, not to mince words, are our rivals in manufacture and in trade, and it is those rivals who have been working for this legislation".[82]

But the bone of contention in the Council was the provision for regulating the labor of adult males. The representatives of several chambers of commerce and associations of millowners as well as other non-partisan members emphatically protested against such an innovation in Indian factory legislation, basing protests on the following arguments: —

First, legal restrictions on adult male labor would seriously injure the industrial development of the country. Sir Vithaldas Damodher Thackersey reiterated his arguments before the commission. He pointed out that, if legislation once undertook to limit the working hours to 12 or 13, further restrictions would be asked by Manchester interests along the same line. He also contended that employers would be deprived of any occasional overtime work, which was necessary in all industries. Hon.

[82] India, Legislative Council Proceedings, Calcutta, 1910—11, 49 : 93.

M. B. Dadabhoy expressed a similar opinion. Referring to the depressing conditions of the nineties, under which certain factories had suffered financial loss, several of them changing hands and many others being sold at auction at one-fifth or one-sixth of the original cost, Mr. Dadabhoy asked if there was no justification under the circumstances for work at high pressure? The employers and employees of Bombay and Agra had to replenish their exhausted resources during the brief period of prosperity. Any other country would have adopted similar methods under similar conditions. Overwork was not unknown in England — a fact which could be verified by the trade reports of Great Britain during the Russo-Japanese War.

Second, the proposed regulation of adult male labor would interfere with the freedom of contract. Mr. Dadabhoy stated that the principle of non-interference with private contract was a recognised canon of enlightened administration. The freedom of capitalists and laborers to enter into an agreement which they thought desirable and mutually advantageous, should be respected, unless it outraged the moral sense of the community. The curtailment of the freedom of action of citizens must always be regarded as a serious encroachment on civic rights. Though Indian labor was unorganized, common action among factory laborers was not unknown. "It is the birthright of everyman", went on Mr. Dadabhoy, "to pursue his own interests in his own way. If there is one principle which is universally acknowledged and respected in all civilised countries, it is the right of the individual to fix of his own free will the hours of work. Every man is the master of his time and energy; their application must be left to be determined by individual volition".[83]

Discussing the proposal, Sir V. D. Thackersey said that further limitation of labor in factories was unnecessary and uncalled for. In the first place, no case had been made out to prove the existence of the sweating system in Indian factories. Extra work meant extra pay

[83] India, Legislative Council Proceedings, Calcutta, 1910—11, 49 : 87.

to employees. In the second place, the health of workers had not been found to suffer from overwork. On the contrary, the vital statistics kept by Dr. Turner for seven years showed that the death rate among factory laborers in Bombay was 18.45 as against 31.58 among general laborers. The death rate in the district of Ratnagiri, whence the Bombay factory laborers came and whither they returned after a few years' work, was the lowest in the whole Presidency of Bombay. In the third place, the overwork was greatly limited in its scope. There were 224 cotton factories in India, but only 100 of them were fitted with electric lights and only 25 or 30 of the latter class had worked excessive hours. For this small number, it was proposed to penalise all of them. If the Government really meant to regulate labor in Indian factories, Sir Vithaldas proposed to accept *in toto* the recommendations of the commission. If the object in view was not thus attained, it would be quite easy for the government to put direct restrictions on adult male labor.

In reply to the objection that the creation of a young person class would increase administrative inconvenience, Sir David Sassoon said that the industrial interests of the country should not be subordinated to administrative convenience. Such inconvenience could be avoided and had been avoided in Great Britain. Mr. Monteath, representing the Bombay Chamber of Commerce, also protested against direct restriction and suggested that the object desired could be secured by adding the following clause to the proposed act: — Provided that in the case of textile factories, in which a system of employment in shifts approved by the local inspector is not in force, there shall be, after the factory has run 12 hours excluding the stoppages under this section, an entire stoppage of all work for not less than one hour in cases where the previous stoppages aggregate not less than one hour, and not less than one hour and a half in cases in which there has been a stoppage of half an hour only.[84]

---

[84] India, Legislative Council Proceedings, Calcutta, 1910—11, 49 : 97.

In reply, Mr. Robertson said for the Government that the success of the proposals of the commission had been doubted by several local governments and others. On the other hand, the importance of limiting hours of work to 12 had been realized even by employers themselves. Shorter hours had been found to have a tendency to increase the output. Many of the shiftless habits of laborers had been ascribed to long hours. The recurrence of the long working hours found by the commission must once and for all be rendered impossible. "Surely it is not to the disadvantage of the mill industry", continued Mr. Robertson, "that Government should step in to do what farseeing factory owners themselves admit to be imperative for the ultimate success of the industry, and that the foundation should be laid for the building up of a highly trained operative class, by work of whose hands the manufacturing wealth of the country will increase."[85]

Passage of the Bill.

On January 31, 1911, Mr. Robertson presented the report of the select committee to the legislative council. Out of sixteen members on the committee, six were non-officials, including the representatives of the Bengal Chamber of Commerce, the Bombay Chamber of Commerce, the Jute Millowners' Association, and the Bombay Millowners' Association as well as the representatives of other industries; and all of them unanimously opposed the provision for direct restriction of adult male labor and added a minute of dissent to the report to that effect.

The other provisions of the bill were based mainly on the recommendations of the commission. The select committee concurred with the commission in its recommendation for doing away with the inspection of factories by ex-officio members, but on the representation of certain local governments that it would be impossible for the expert inspectors to visit out-of-the-way places regularly, provision was made in the bill for the appointment of

[85] India, Legislative Council Proceedings, Calcutta 1910—11, 49 : 101.

additional inspectors, where such was considered necessary. In such cases, it was not considered advisable to give the additional inspectors full powers under the act, and a clause was, therefore, inserted enabling local governments to define the powers which they were to exercise. Another change in the bill gave employers power to appeal to local governments against the orders of inspectors. The local governments, in such cases, were to appoint an official, who, assisted by expert assessors, should hear the case. The bill made provision for the appointment of such assessors.[86]

On March 21, 1911, a motion was made in the Indian Legislative Council by Hon. W. H. Clark, member from the Department of Commerce and Industry, for final consideration of the bill to consolidate and amend the law regulating labor in factories. He announced that the bill was non-contentious except in the part which related to the labor in textile factories and that there were three amendments to that part.

As in the former case, the main issue was raised about legislative regulation of adult male labor. Sir Vithaldas, as the spokesman of his non-official colleagues on the select committee, again protested against the introduction of such a novel measure into Indian factory legislation. He said that there was no difference of opinion regarding the necessity of limiting the working hours of factory workers. But the main question was how to attain the desired object. If the government doubted the success of the commission's proposals, he would suggest an ammendment, which, if adopted, would accomplish the same thing as the Government had in view without imposing any direct restrictions on the hours of adult male laborers. Provision had already been made to limit the working hours of a factory from 5.30 A. M. to 7 P. M. with an interval of rest for half an hour after 6 hours of work. If it were made compulsory that a factory must stop work for one hour after 12 hours' work, no factory could

[86] India, Legislative Council Proceedings, Calcutta, 1910—1911, 49 : 218—19.

work more than 12 hours. Sir Vithaldas affirmed that the new proposal by the Government had caused great alarm in the industrial community. The history of the excise duty on Indian cotton factories impressed upon the people of the country the fact that, if the direct restrictions on adult male labor were once resorted to, sooner or later, outside pressure would be brought upon the Government for further concession along the same lines, and the Government, with all the good will in the world, would be powerless to resist. The Government, therefore, by adopting the new method, should not throw away a valuable safeguard to the interest of Indian industries.

Sir Vithaldas was followed by Mr. Dadabhoy, who again unhesitatingly condemned the revision of the bill. He questioned the accuracy of the statement by Mr. Robertson that shorter hours had the tendency to increase the output — a thing doubted by the commission itself. He was not sanguine about the improvement of general health and conditions of life of the laboring classes by restricting the hours of labor to 12, and, in support of his view, he quoted the opinion of the Upper India Chamber of Commerce. On the other hand, this restriction would strangle Indian industry by seriously handicapping Indian manufacturers in their competition with China and Japan. Finally, he reiterated the argument of Sir Vithaldas that this regulation would serve only as a prelude to further regulation of a similar kind.

Rao Bahadur Mudholkar also revoiced his protest against the provision and, in the course of his speech, pointed out the difficulties which the Indian textile industry had to suffer; machinery had to be obtained from abroad, capital in India was comparatively limited, and laborers were ignorant, untrained and inefficient. Even the overseers and managers were not as highly qualified as those in Europe and America. The result was that the cost of production was greater in India. These difficulties were increased by scarcity of labor during times of plague and epidemics. Under these circumstances, it was employers, and not employees, who were at a disadvantage. "It is on a consideration of practical difficulties like these," concluded Mr. Mudholkar, "not on mere abstract grounds of the doctrine of laissez faire, that legislative interference with adult male labor is deprecated."[87]

There were two other points on which Sir Vithaldas differed from the majority of the select committee and opposed the provisions of the bill thereon. First, he objected, as before in the commission, to the extension of the provisions of the bill to factories working daylight hours. The contention that daylight hours would extend to 14 or 14½ in the hottest period of the year would be met by his amendment, under which the working day should not exceed 12½ hours. The Bombay Government was in favor of this proposition. Second, he objected to the Government's omission from the bill of the recommendation of the commission for the appointment of a chief inspector of factories, the primary object of which was to insure uniformity in the administration of the factory law. In case the decision of the Government remained unchanged, he suggested that the Government should draw up a set of model rules for the guidance of the local governments, which would make the necessary changes in them according to local requirements. He further suggested the holding of an annual conference of factory inspectors to compare notes with a view to keeping factory administration on the same level of efficiency in all parts of the country.

Following the discussion, several amendments were proposed by the members. The first amendment moved by Sir Vithaldas provided that every textile factory after working 12 hours should stop work for one hour, as stated in his discussion. The proposal was opposed by the Government on the ground of administrative difficulties in factories working on the shift system and negatived by the Council.

Hon. Archey Birkmyre followed Sir Vithaldas with two amendments. His proposals were first, to begin work

[87] India, Legislative Council, Proceedings, Calcutta, 1910—11. 49 : 586.

at 6 A. M. instead of 5.30 A. M. and stop at 7 P. M., and second, to increase the working hours of children from 6 to 6½, so that cotton factories could work 13 hours with two shifts of children, but the work of adult males would not exceed 12 hours. With a proper arrangement of shifts, each employee might be worked 10 hours. In support of his proposals, he said that the object of limiting hours of work to 12, could be achieved by this method without having resort to any drastic measure proposed by the Government, that the shorter work period of 13 hours would render inspection easier and that at the same time the commencement of work at 6 A. M. instead of 5.30 A. M. would be beneficial to employees. In support of the second proposal, he argued that evil effects of work on children were not due to 7 hours' work as prescribed by the existing law, but to the abuses of longer hours in violation of the legal limit, the employment of underaged children, etc., which had been made possible through inadequacy of inspection and absence of compulsory certification. Finally, he said that the Government of Bengal approved of the proposed longer hours. The proposals were refused consideration on three grounds: — first, administrative difficulties; second, disapproval of them by all the local governments other than the Bengal; third, recommendation of the commission not to increase the working hours of children more than 6 in any one day. The amendments were, therefore, withdrawn.

The next amendment was moved by Mr. Gokhale, who proposed that in all factories employing more than 20 children, the children between the ages of 9 and 12 should be given 3 hours of free and compulsory education. He supported his proposal on the ground of both justice and humanity. The employment of children in factories prevented them from availing themselves of the existing facilities for receiving instruction at school. The parents, because of employment in factories, could not exercise necessary supervision over their children. Children also deserved humane consideration, as they were least able to take care of themselves. The proposal was objected to by Mr. Dadabhoy on the ground that education was the duty of the State and not of factory owners, and also by Mr. Madge on the ground that the addition of 3 hours' study to 6 hours' work would be fatal to the health of the children. The Government raised 3 objections to the proposal: — First, schools set up within the borders of a factory would not secure efficient education. Second, it would not be fair to place such a burden on factories. Third, it might lead to abuses of the law regarding the limitations of the hours of child labor. The proposal was withdrawn.

The third amendment, or set of amendments, was brought in by Mr. Mudholkar, who proposed to exclude the factories working daylight hours from the operation of the contended provision on condition that the maximum amount of work should not exceed 12½ hours in any one day and the average period of work should not be more than 12 hours a day in a year. Sir Vithaldas supported the proposal, saying that under this system many factories would be absolved from the installation of electric light. Mr. Gokhale also supported the proposal on the ground that, in the interest of operatives themselves, such an arrangement would be better than the one proposed by the Government of a rigid 12 hours a day. They understood it better and it was also less liable to abuse. The Government opposed the proposal, advancing several reasons: — First, the longest time of work would have to be done in the hottest period of the season. Second, it would increase the work of children from 6 hours to 6¼, and that during the hottest period of the year. Third, it would not be of any substantial benefit to millowners. Fourth, it would increase administrative difficulty. And fifth, the argument that employees liked daylight hours in preference to any definite and fixed period of 12 hours had been misrepresented. What they objected to was the work by electric light, which they understood to be the same as long hours. The proposal was negatived by the Council and the bill, as reported by the select committee, was passed on the same day. The act was called the "Indian Factories Act, 1911", being Act No. XII of 1911, and came into force on July 1, 1912.

Chief Provisions of the Act:

1. The age limits of children for employment were put between 9 and 14 years as before. They were, however, required to produce the certificate of age and physical fitness.

2. The working hours of children and women were limited to 7 and 11 respectively. In textile factories, children were permitted to work only 6 hours and adult males to work 12 hours in any one day.

3. The working time for children, women and adult men in textile factories were limited to the period between 5.30 A. M. and 7 P. M.

4. Textile factories were prohibited from using any mechanical and electrical power for more than 12 hours in a day.

5. Factories had to make arrangement for ventilation, lighting, fire-escapes, water-supply, etc. Children and women were prohibited from being employed in certain dangerous work.

6. All factories were required to stop work for at least half an hour after every 6 hours' work.

CHAPTER V.

FACTORY ACT OF 1922.

The Political Movement.

Not long after the enactment of the third factory act, the world was plunged into the great European conflict, in which India had to take a prominent part on the side of the Allies. Like many other nations, India underwent complete political and economic changes during the war. The chief forces which brought about and molded the first three factory acts lost their momentum, and a new political and economic consciousness among the people formed an altogether different background for factory legislation.

The most important change in the national life of India was the rise of a new political ideal. The national movement which first asserted itself in the protest against the partition of Bengal in 1905, after a decade of many viscissitudes, emerged as a great national force during the early part of the war. India's participation in the war was followed by a demand from her for full citizenship in the British commonwealth. In 1915, Hindus and Mohammedans who had been kept apart for a long time, adjusted their differences, and when, in 1916, nineteen members of the Imperial Legislative Council drew up a scheme by which the executive was to be subordinated to the legislature, both the Indian National Congress and the All-India Muslim League took it as the minimum demand upon the British Government. The Home Rule movement was in full swing in 1917. There soon followed a series of important events, such as the prosecution of Mr. Gandhi for his championship of the laborers' cause in their grievances against British indigo planters in Bihar, the internment of Home Rule "agitators" in Madras and the Punjab, the Rowlatt Acts, the Jallianwalla Bagh massacre, and the dismemberment of Turkey in which one fifth of the people of India professing the Mohammedan faith was vitally interested. These occurrences stirred the people throughout the length and breadth of the country and led to the rise of the non-cooperation movement. Thus, what was only the "agitation" of the "intellectuals" a few years ago became a mighty movement of the millions of the masses under the leadership of Mr. Gandhi. The movement for Swadeshi or the consumption of goods made in the country, was transformed into the movement for Swaraj, or national government.

With the transformation in the political consciousness, there also took place a change in the constitution of the Government of India. At the beginning of the war practically all parties supported the Government in the prosecution of it. In recognition of India's contribution to the defence of the British Empire, it was declared from the throne on August 20, 1917, that India would be granted an opportunity for "the progressive realization of a reponsible government" as "an integral part of the British Empire". Acting upon this declaration, the Secretary of State for India and the Viceroy made a report in July, 1918, on a scheme for a new constitution. The new constitution was adopted, with some modifications, in the British Parliament in December, 1919, and became operative at the beginning of 1921. This constitution granted the people certain powers in some minor or "reserved" subjects of the Provincial Governments, and also provided for somewhat better representation in the Central Government. Many important subjects, however, including the budget, both in the provincial and central governments are still entirely outside the control of the people.

The nationalists, who form by far the majority of the people in India, have altogether repudiated the new constitution. The moderates, while not altogether satisfied with its provisions, have accepted it as a temporary measure. The new constitution, with a legislature of two chambers, Council of State and Legislative Assembly, is nevertheless an improvement in so far as it gives the people a better channel for voicing their opinions on national questions.

The rise of the new political consciousness, reinforced by the reforms in the constitution has, as stated before, brought about a new situation in the country. There has appeared an intelligent public which is both critical and constructive on the one hand, and alert and aggressive for the defence of its rights and interests on the other. Irrespective of their political creeds, the Moderates and Nationalists are agreed upon one point — that there shall be no interference from outside in questions concerning purely internal affairs. They are determined that henceforth outside influence shall play a role less and less important in the legislation of the country, and that the labor law shall be enacted by the Indian people themselves.

The Industrial Movement.

Along with the political movement, there has also appeared a vigorous movement for industrial development. Soon after the introduction of the factory system, some two generations ago, Indian capitalists began to take initiative in modern methods of production. But it was not until 1905 that the attention of the nation as a whole was drawn to the importance of industrial development. In that year, as mentioned before, the Bengalees boycotted British goods. The Boycott was soon turned into Swadeshi. The boycott failed and even Swadeshi lost its momentum for a period until revived in 1918 by Mr. Gandhi. But the national consciousness has now been fully awakened to the necessity of making supreme efforts to advance the industrial interests of India by the Indians themselves.

This industrial awakening of the people, moreover, has been accompanied by a change in the industrial policy of the Government. In spite of the desultory attempts of some local governments, such as those in Madras in the nineties, and in the United Provinces in 1907, the Government of India was indifferent to the necessity of developing the manufacturing industries of the country. The efforts of Lord Morley in 1910 and of Lord Crewe in 1912, did not bear any fruit.[1] But the Great War brought home to the British Government the important truth that even for the defence of the British Empire, the development of India's resources was absolutely necessary. The realization of this fact led the British Government to change its policy and appoint a commission on May 19, 1916, to "examine and report upon the possibility of further industrial development in India."[2] After two years of investigation, the commission made its final report on the methods of developing the industries of India in 1918. The Government at once gave effect to some of these recommendations.

Whether the Government will accept principles that the Indian people believe to be required by the national economy of India and adopt a policy by which the resources of India will be developed by Indians and for the Indian people, remains to be seen. But India has already entered into a new industrial career.

Soon after the outbreak of the war, imports into India from European countries, especially from Great Britain and Germany, were perceptibly reduced or completely cut off. India had to supply the Allies with arms, ammunition and other war materials. Being compelled to depend upon herself for many commodities she had hitherto imported from abroad, and having also to produce for export, India devoted herself to the development of manufacturing industries. The enormous profits made by several industries led their promoters to expand their industrial enterprises. Also many new manufacturing industries, such as tanning and oil-pressing, were started. The Indian public has come to the assistance of the capitalists by investing in new industrial ventures. While in 9 months' period from April to December, 1918, the number of industrial companies registered was only 158 with a capital of £ 4,500,000, during 12 months of 1919—20, no less

---

[1] The Report of the Indian Industrial Commission, 1916—18, London, 1919, Cmd. 51, pp. 68—72.

[2] Ibid., p. 1.

than 906 such companies were floated and their aggregate capital amounted to £ 183,000,000.[3]

The industries which made the largest profits were those related to cotton, jute, and iron. In the jute industry, the ratio of profits to the total paid up capital for the first half year of 1918 rose to 73 per cent. The aggregate total profit — after the deduction of interest on investment, for 36 concerns, was Rs. 71,885,000.[4] A similar advance in profit is shown in the case of the cotton industry. From an average annual income of 17,400,000 rupees for the decade from 1905 to 1914, it rose to 130,600,000 rupees in 1919.[5] Even in the year 1920 when there was a general slump in the cotton industry all over the world, and a large number of strikes occurred in this industry in India itself, the cotton industry in India showed an "unprecedented" and "unparallelled" prosperity. The profits of the Bombay mills alone were estimated to be Rs. 160,000,000. About 40 per cent of the internal demand for cotton goods in India is now supplied by the factories of India. Moreover, her production in the cotton goods of finer counts has also increased and these became a "constant encroachment upon Lancashire Trade."[7]

The result of this industrial development has been that there has already grown up in India a well-organized capitalist class among the Indians themselves, which is not only quite capable of undertaking some of the greatest industrial enterprises of modern times, but is also powerful enough to influence the industrial policy of the government and to counteract the foreign influence so detrimental to India's interest.

[3] India in 1919, Calcutta, 1920, p. 78.

[4] The Times Trade Supplement, London, March 3, 1919, p. 285.

[5] Ibid., Nov. 6, 1920, p. 178. Computed.

[6] Ibid., May 14, 1921, p. 169.

[7] Gt. Brit. Parliamentary Debates, 1917, 91 : 1165.

Agitation for Import Duties.

In the meantime, under the stress of the war expenditure, Great Britain found it necessary to call upon her colonies and dependencies for financial help. India, whose contribution and sacrifice were very great, proposed in the Legislative Council as early as September, 1914, that she would share in the heavy financial burden then imposed by the war on the United Kingdom.[8] Later on, India made an offer of £ 100,000,000 towards the expenses of the war. In order to maintain the interest and sinking fund on the gift, it became necessary for her to levy new and additional taxes and to increase her customs duties.

It should be remembered that early in the nineties, when fiscal difficulties drove the Government of India to the re-imposition of import duties on cotton goods, the Lancashire interests raised a strong protest and compelled the Government to levy an equivalent excise duty on cotton goods manufactured in India. As a result of this duty, not only Indian goods competing with those of Lancashire were put under disadvantage, but the manufacture of any kind of cotton was restricted. While the extremists called this "a glaring example of British exploitation of India", the moderates regarded it "unfair" and "unjust". Ever since, this excise duty has been one of the greatest sources of irritation and agitation among all classes of people.

At the first realization of the fact that she would have to meet the expenses of the compaign she herself undertook in the Eastern theatre of the war and also to contribute to the imperial war funds, India thought of reforming her tariff and of raising her import duties on all goods including cotton manufactures. Even as early as May 13, 1916, the Statesman, an Anglo-Indian newspaper, gave the warning that the ultimate object of all tariff reform was to "impose increasing burdens upon British exports and especially on Lancashire goods."[10] But when the import

---

[8] Gt. Brit. Parliamentary Debates, 1917, H. of C. 91 : 1138.
[9] Ibid., 1917, H. of C. 24 : 556.
[10] Ibid., 1917, H. of C. 91 : 1214. Quoted by Mr. Denniss.

duty on Lancashire goods was raised from 3½ to 7½ per cent without increasing the countervailing excise duty on Indian cotton manufactures, Lancashire raised a storm of protest.[11]

On March 5, 1917, Mr. W. Barton asked the Secretary of State for India whether the increase of 4 per cent duty on cotton goods imported into India was to be accompanied by a corresponding increase in the excise duty then levied on cotton goods manufactured in India. On March 12, 1917, an influential deputation representing employers and employees in the cotton trade of Lancashire waited upon the Secretary of State for India and strongly objected to the action which had been taken. The Secretary did not see any serious competition on the part of India and pointed out the attitude of the Indian people on the question of excise duty.[12] On March 13, 1917, the same deputation again waited upon the Prime Minister who observed that under ordinary circumstances the case of the deputation would have been irrefutable but that nothing could be done in view of the prevailing situation.[13] On March 14, 1917, the Lancashire interests bitterly attacked the British Government for allowing the India Government to raise the import duties on their cotton goods without a countervailing excise duty on the Indian cotton manufactures. Although it was promised that the whole question of tariff reform in the Empire would be reopened at the close of the war, all the Chambers of Commerce in Lancashire passed resolutions asking his Majesty's Government "to take immediate steps to postpone such a controversial measure until after the war."[14] But His Majesty's Government failed to take any action and the Government of India did not revoke its decision. Thus after dictating the terms of Indian tariff for about two generations in order to control the Indian markets, the Manchester interests for the first time met with defeat.

---

[11] Gt. Brit. Parliamentary Debates, 1917, H. of C. 91 : 1156.
[12] Ibid., 24 : 520.
[13] Ibid., 91 : 1163—64.
[14] Ibid., 91 : 1198.

This defeat of the Lancashire interests in the control of Indian import duties was followed by a similar defeat in their interference with factory legislation in India. On March 14, 1917, the Secretary of State for India refused to mix two entirely distinct subjects, namely, import duties on Lancashire manufactures imported into India and the factory laws which ought to prevail there.[15] On April 4, 1917, Mr. L. Haslam asked in the House of Commons whether the Secretary of State for India would make representation to the Government of India stating the desirability of shortening the hours of work in Indian factories so that children of 9 years of age should not be permitted by law to work 6 hours a day, and that the hours of work for women should not be longer than those permitted in the United Kingdom. The Secretary of State did not see any reason for acting according to these suggestions.[16] On March 11, 1919, Mr. Haslam repeated the question and was told that that was not an opportune time for inviting the Government of India to undertake fresh factory legislation.[17]

The Industrial Commission of 1916—18.

Mention has already been made of the appointment of the Industrial Commission by the Government of India, which, after two years' inquiry made several recommendations for further industrial development. One of the important subjects into which the commission investigated was the conditions of labor, especially those related to health, housing and education.

The commission came to the conclusion that the laborers in the organised industries of India were less efficient than the corresponding classes of laborers in the Western countries. One of the reasons for such inefficiency was that the conditions under which the workers lived and worked in India were much worse than those prevailing in the Western countries. "No industrial edifice can be permanent," observed the commission, "which is built

---

[15] Gt. Brit. Parliamentary Debates, H. of C, 1917, 91 : 1143.
[16] Ibid., 92 : 1411—12.
[17] Ibid., H. of C., 1919, 113 : 1112.

on such unsound foundations as those afforded by Indian labor under its present conditions".[18]

The commission recommended the establishment of sanitary organisations for improving public health and for combating many preventable diseases to which Indian laborers and the people usually fell victims. Public health was also dependent upon housing conditions, for the betterment of which the commission recommended that the dwellings built by employers in industrial centres must be of a type approved by the local sanitary authorities, and the land required for accommodating laborers should be acquired, if necessary, by the Government or local authorities, and sold or leased to employers. A permanent body of workers was necessary for the development of efficiency. The commission recommended the introduction of compulsory education for all children in factory areas, and the amendment of the factory act, requiring the attendance of school by all factory children. "If the workers' children", observed the commission, "are provided with education under tolerable conditions of life, a new generation of workers will grow up, who will learn to regard factory work as their fixed occupation."[19]

In the case of Bombay, however, the existing congestion and the difficulties in the way of betterment were so unique that the commission made two special recommendations: First, that the future congestion of the city should be avoided by prohibiting the establishment of new industrial concerns without special permission of the municipality. Second, that the existing state of affairs must be improved by adopting a definite standard of industrial dwellings to be taken up and worked out at the expense of the local authorities, which, if necessary, might seek the assistance of the local government and even impose tax on employers.

The commission could not, however, recommend any reduction in the hours of factory work. The workers

---

[18] Report of the Indian Industrial Commission, 1916—18, London, 1919, Cmd. 51, p. 151.

[19] Ibid., p. 151.

loitered away much of the time during which they were nominally at work and did not learn how to use a longer period of leisure more advantageously, such a "concession" might not be an "unmixed" benefit. The commission realised the importance of welfare work, but did not make any definite suggestion. "The direct participation of official agency in social welfare work", concluded the commission, "must wait until the civic sense has become more fully developed.[20]

The First International Labor Conference.

In the meantime, the Great War came to a close and the Peace Conference at Paris appointed a representative commission early in 1919 to inquire into the conditions of employment in different countries, to suggest international measures for securing common action on matters affecting the conditions of employment, and to recommend a form of permanent agency for continuing such inquiry and action. The commission after due consideration presented its report at a plenary session of the Peace Conference in April, 1919, and recommended the establishment of a permanent international labor organization. After an amendment had been made that the conference should have due regard to the climatic and industrial conditions of each country, provided for by Article 405 of the Versailles Treaty of Peace, the proposals of the commission were accepted on behalf of India by Lord Sinha, then the Under Secretary of State for India.

The proposals regarding the betterment of the conditions of labor in different countries were finally embodied in the Peace Treaty and the League of Nations. The first clause of Article 23 of the Covenant of the League of Nations says that the member nations will endeavor "to secure and maintain fair humane conditions of labor", and to this end, "establish and maintain necessary international organizations." The International Labor Organization thus constituted consists of two branches: First, an International Labor Office to be con-

[20] Report of the Indian Industrial Commission, 1916—18, London, 1919, Cmd. 51, p. 161.

trolled by a governing body. Second, a General Conference of representatives of the members of the League.

The actions which are obligatory on all members of the League are embodied in Article 405 of the Peace Treaty. Each State on receipt of the proposals of the Labor Organization or of the Labor Conference, is bound to place them before the proper authorities for legislation or other action. The conference meets every year and has two functions: (1) Recommendations and (2) Draft Conventions. In the case of recommendations, each member State has only to report to the secretary general of the League of Nations as to the action taken. In the case of draft conventions, the member State will, if it obtains the consent of the authority or authorities within whose competence the matter lies, communicate the formal ratification of the conventions to the secretary general and will take such action as may be necessary to make effective the provisions of such conventons.[21]

On April 11th, 1919, the Peace Conference approved, with some changes, the standing orders of the International Labor Organization proposed by its commission on international labor legislation. The first meeting of the conference was held at Washington, D. C., from October 29 to November 29, 1919. The following provisions were under consideration: — (1) Application of the principle of the 8 hour day or the 48 hour week. (2) Question of preventing or providing against unemployment. (3) Women's employment: (a) before and after childbirth (including the question of maternity benefit; (b) during the night, (including the Berne convention of 1906 on night work for women), and in unhealthy processes. (4) Employment of children: (a) minimum age of admission; (b) during the night; (c) in unhealthy processes. (5) Extension and application of the international convention adopted at Berne in 1906 on the prohibition of the use of white phosphorous in the manufacture of matches.[22]

---

[21] Treaty with Germany, June 28, 1919, Washington, 1919, Art. 405, p. 160.

[22] First International Labor Conference, Washington, D. C., 1920, p. 14.

At the meeting India was represented by Mr. L. J. Kershaw and Mr. A. C. Chatterjee for the Government, by Sir A. R. Murray for employers, and by Mr. N. M. Joshi for labor. Mr. B. P. Wadia, President, Madras Labor Union, was the adviser for labor.

The conference divided its work among different commissions and committees for the formulation of recommendations and draft conventions. There were altogether 6 conventions and 6 recommendations on the subjects on which the Conference was called upon to give its opinion. The questions which were of special importance to India centered around the hours of work and the minimum age for children.

The question of the working hours was discussed in great detail by a commission appointed by the conference. Under Article 405 of the Treaty of Peace, the case of the countries claiming special consideration was taken up. It was decided that the hours of work in India might be reduced from 72 to 60 a week.

Mr. Joshi proposed that the following amendment be made to the proposed convention: First, the word "factory" to be applied to India should mean "any industry worked with steam, water, or any other mechanical or electrical power and employing not less than 10 persons." Second, the hours of work for women employed in factories should not exceed 54 a week. Third, that children under 14 years of age should not be employed for more than 30 hours a week.[23] The amendment was rejected.

The Commission, however, recommended asking the Government of India to adopt the principle of a 60 hour week and to consider the possibility of introducing a 54 hour week or even a shorter one in the mines, and of modifying the definition of "factory" so as to apply it to the premises where fewer than 50 persons were employed.[24]

---

[23] First, International Labor Conference, Washington, D. C., 1920, pp. 167—169—267.

[24] Ibid., p. 231.

On the question of the minimum age of children, he Government of India instructed its delegates to the conference to vote against any increase. The conference appointed a sub-committee to report on modifications necessary because of the climatic and industrial conditions of oriental countries. Mr. Joshi recommended the desirability of raising the minimum age, but both the committee and the commission rejected the proposition on the ground that the Government of India still had the question under consideration. When the question came up for deliberation in the conference, Miss Margaret Bonfield, one of the advisers of the labor delegates from Great Britain, proposed for India and other oriental countries that the minimum age of children for employment should be fixed at 12 in factories working with power and employing more than 10 persons, in mines and quarries, and on railroads and docks. The chief aim of this resolution was to give India some idea of the world's opinion. The resolution was supported by Mr. Joshi and carried.[25]

The Labor Movement.[26]

Meantime a new force has made its appearance in the industrial life of India. The labor movement which was started in 1875, has become today a strong social, political and industrial force. Following the formation of a trade union in Madras by Mr. B. P. Wadia in 1918, industrial unions began to spring up all over the country. In 1919 the workers of Bombay held a labor conference which was attended by representatives from 75 factories. This conference drew up a memorandum of demands upon employers. By 1920 practically all the trades in India were organized and an All-India Trade Union Congress was formed under competent leadership.

The immediate objects of the labor movement are an increase in wages, shorter hours of work, and better work-

[25] First, International Labor Conference, Washington, 1919, Washington, 1920, pp. 93—97.
[26] Cf., Das, R. K., Factory Labor in India, chap. 10.

ing and housing conditions. But it has also been actuated by some broader aims and higher ideals, such as education and training, social betterment, political enfranchisement, and even universal brotherhood.

For the realization of their aims and ideals, the workers have adopted various means, such as social centers and evening schools. The strike is, however, their most effective weapon, and this they have used especially for achieving their more immediate objects. In 1919—20 they organized strike after strike and paralyzed industrial organization in many parts of the country. For the purpose of securing a 60 hour week in the place of the existing 72 hour week and of increasing the minimum age of children for admission into factories, they called about 200,000 persons out of the factories and workshops of Bombay and kept them out for several weeks. The demand for shorter hours was granted by employers in Bombay as well as in many of the other industrial centers.

The effect of the organization of labor is that instead of being the incoherent and unorganized mass of individuals of a few years ago, Indian laborers are today a well-organized and consolidated body, fully alive to their own interests. It is true that they still depend upon outsiders for leadership as was the case in the beginning of the labor movement in other countries. The outstanding features of the movement in India today are: — First, the laborers have a practical program for the furtherance of their own welfare. Second, they are more capable of taking a common stand against any encroachment on their interests. Third, they have won the sympathy of the public to their cause. Fourth, they have also influenced the Government to support some of their demands. In the present legislature where vital labor laws are being framed, they have their own representative to plead their cause. On March 1, 1921, a resolution was also passed in the Legislative Assembly recommending to the Governor General in Council to introduce in the legislature such measure as might be necessary for the registration of trade unions.[27]

[27] India, Legislative Assembly Debates, 1921, I.: 486—506.

Growth of Public Opinion.

Meanwhile an intelligent public opinion on industrial and labor questions has also been created. The strikes stirred up the public interest in the labor question. Newspapers and periodicals devoted considerable space to descriptions of labor conditions including the hours of work, standards of living, and housing conditions.[28] Research and investigations into labor conditions were undertaken by scientists and philanthropists, and the results of these studies were published in the organs of such social and economic associations as the Indian Economic Association and the Servants of India Society. These associations also devoted a good deal of time in their meetings and conventions to the discussion of labor problems.

The public gradually took a more sympathetic attitude toward labor. Shorter hours, higher wages, improvement of housing conditions, increase in the minimum age of children for admission into factories, minimum wage, and compulsory education were advocated publicly. On February 19, 1920, the Hon. Khan Bahadur E. H. Jaffer made a motion in the Legislative Council to appoint a commission to inquire into the conditions of factory labor and to consider the desirability of establishing courts of arbitration for the settlement of industrial disputes. Referring to the over-crowding, insanitary dwelling, insufficient wages, and recent industrial unrest, he advocated the remedy for some of these problems by legislation. It was only when the Government of India declared that the recommendations of the Industrial Commission and also the conventions and recommendations of the first International Labor Conference had been under consideration

---

[28] The *Bombay Chronicle* took the lead in bringing the problems of labor before the public. The *labor* cause was also taken up by such newspapers as the *Hindu*, the *New India* at Madras, the *Tribune* at Lahore, and the *Amritabazar Patrika* at Calcutta. Periodicals such as the *Modern Review* and the *Indian Review* began to publish articles on the labor question and labor legislation.

for some time and that the Government would soon give effect to them that the resolution was withdrawn.[29]

This new social consciousness did not fail in exerting some influence on the capitalistic class. Even before the Washington Conference made its recommendations, the matter of shortening working hours had engaged the attention of Bombay millowners. They felt that the hours of work were too long and later on, when the demand for shorter hours came from laborers also, they at once granted it. In order to make the shorter work day general in India, the Bombay Millowners' Association, in March, 1920, presented a memorial to His Excellency the Viceroy in which they pointed out that one of the demands made by mill operatives in Bombay, when they went on strike in January of 1920, was a reduction of mill hours from 12 to 10 a day, and they requested the Governor General in Council to amend the factory act.[30]

While the representation was being made to the Government for legislation to shorten the working day, most of the factories adopted a 60 hour week. A 10 hour day was adopted in the Buckingham and Carnatic Mills of Madras, and 10 hours also became the nominal working day at Dhariwal, at Nagpur and elsewhere, and many factories observed still shorter hours.[31] Thus, a 10 hour day became a fact long before it became a law.

The Ratification of the Washington Conventions.

The recommendations of the Industrial Commission of 1916—18 were given serious consideration by the Government of India which issued, in June, 1919, a circular letter to local governments and called their attention to the recommendations regarding education, housing, and social welfare upon which depended the prospects of improving the efficiency of labor.[32]

---

[29] India, Legislative Council Proceedings, Calcutta, 1920, 48 : 808—19.

[30] India, Legislative Assembly Debates, 1921, 1 : 252.

[31] Ibid., p. 252.

[32] India, Legislative Council Proceedings, Calcutta, 1920, 48 : 814—15.

In the meantime, the first International Labor Conference at Washington D. C., coming to a close, the Government of India also proceeded to obtain the views of the local governments and of public bodies as to the advisibility of ratifying them.

In February, 1920, the nature of the conventions was discussed in the Legislative Council and it was announced that the matter would soon come up for disposal.[33] On the 10th of March following, it was stated in the British Parliament in reply to a question by Mr. A. Short, that the ratification of the conventions and recommendations would soon be brought up in the Indian Legislature. Up to that time the Government of India had not, however, come to a final decision on all of the points.[34] In May, 1920, the Indian Government, while realising the importance of giving effect to the conventions on the age limit of children, pointed out the danger of depriving children of 9 to 12 years of age of the training which they received in factories when there were no corresponding facilities for education.[35]

Meanwhile, the International Labor Conference held its second annual meeting at Genoa from June 15 to July 10, 1920,[36] in which a draft convention was passed providing that children under the age of 14 years should not be employed on vessels other than those upon which other members of the same family were employed.[37]

It was proposed in a discussion on June 29, that no seaman under 18 might be employed as a trimmer or stoker. Mr. L. Kershaw, the Indian Government's representative, proposed an amendment to the effect that in British India the convention should be applied in the sense that no person under the age of 12 be employed on deck or saloon crews. Most of the Indian children working at sea accompanied their parents. Mr. Kershaw's amending proposition was rejected and at the same time

---

[33] India, Legislative Assembly Debates, 1921, 1:259.
[34] Gt. Brit. Parliamentary Debates, 1920, H. of C. 126:1253.
[35] India, Council of State Debates, 1921, 1:181.
[36] The Times, London, 1920, July 1, p. 15, c. 6.
[37] Gt. Brit. Parl. Papers, 1920, Cmd. 1174, p. 8.

the resolution itself was postponed and referred to the agenda of the next International Labor Conference.[38]

While the opinion of the outside world expressed in the labor conferences and Parliamentary discussions as regards shortening the working hours, increasing the minimum age of children in industry, and other improvements of labor conditions were exerting an influence, the internal forces, such as the labor movement, public opinion, and even some of the employers' organizations, were pressing the Government of India to amend the factory act, as has already been said. The Government of India gradually changed its views and, on November 25, 1920, sent a dispatch to the Secretary of State expressing its intention to recommend the raising of the minimum age of children from 9 to 12 years. Although most of the local governments had recognized that it would be advantageous to raise the minimum age, there were some which were opposed to such action. The Government of India had nevertheless come to the decision because international obligations made it impossible to advocate any lower age.[39] Approval was soon given the measure by the Secretary of State for India and the Government of India reached its final conclusion by the middle of December, 1920.[40]

The question of the ratification of the draft conventions of the first International Labor Conference was finally taken up in the newly constituted Legislative Assembly on February 19, 1921, and in the Council of State on February 21, 1921.

The draft convention secured in the first place a 60 hour maximum week for all workers in factories, in mines and in mechanical transportation services. In the second place, it provided for a maximum of overtime hours, established by public authority after consultation with

[38] The Labor Gazette, Ottawa, Oct. 1920, p. 1320.

[39] India, Council of State Debates, 1921, 1 : 182.

[40] The Times, London, Dec. 23, 1920, p. 9. It must be mentioned that the Bengal Chamber of Commerce was unanimous that there should be no change in the age limit fixed by law. India, Council of State Debates, 1921, 1 : 193.

employers' and workers' organizations, if they existed, and this limitation of overtime might be applied to exceptional industries in which overtime rates of pay of not less than one quarter of the regular rate were provided. The acceptance of the conventions by the Government of India, therefore, meant three things, as pointed out by Mr. A. C. Chatterjee, who moved the resolution in the Council of State: (1) A 60 hour week as maximum; (2) The fixation of the maximum for overtime work according to the interest of each trade and (3) a minimum rate of pay for overtime.

In the discussion of the subject in the legislature, several important points were brought out. Sir Maneckji Dadabhoy gave warning in the Council of State that the 60 hour week would be regarded as the final reduction.[41] On the other hand, Mr. Bhugri in the same chamber would have liked to reduce the hours to 48 a week.[42] Mr. Jamnadas Dwarkadas in the assembly stated that the 10 hour day was "only the first step toward the desideratum of an 8 hour day."[43] Mr. N. M. Joshi criticised the principle of the Labor Conference meeting at Washington for treating men and women alike and for fixing 60 hours a week for both, as noted above. He was in favor of a 54 hour week for women.[44] After much discussion a resolution recommending the Government of India to ratify the convention was passed.

The convention of the Washington Conference regarding unemployment and employment agencies required: (1) the supply by the Government of India to the International Labor Office of all information as to the existence of unemployment. (2) the establishment of free public employment agencies under the control of a central authority with an advisory board which would include representatives of employers and employees.

In addition to the compulsory provisions of the conventions, the Conference recommended also: — (1) that

---

[41] India, Council of State Debates, 1921, 1 : 161.
[42] Ibid., p. 160.
[43] India, Legislative Assembly Debates, 1921, 1 : 260.
[44] Ibid., 1 : 253.

the employment agencies which charged fees and carried on their business for profit should be prohibited; (2) that the recruiting of workers in one country with a view to employment in another should be permitted only by mutual agreement between the countries concerned and only after consultation with employers and workers in each country; (3) that an effective system of unemployment insurance should be established; (4) that the State should coordinate the execution of all work undertaken under public authority, with a view to reserving such work, as far as practicable, for periods of unemployment and for districts most affected by it.[45]

It was pointed out that the conditions in India differed from those in other countries in several ways: — First, in India, the employer sought the worker, not the worker the employment. Second, the workers in India were not in a position to become advisors because of their lack of training and experience.

As far as unemployment was concerned, the Government of India claimed that it had a system of famine administration which had been improved after every famine or scarcity in the last two generations, and which was capable of dealing economically with unemployment on a scale for which few Western countries could offer a parallel.[46] But as long as labor was more congested in certain areas of India than in others, the Government consented to create regular public service agencies to meet this difficulty.

As for the recommendation on unemployment insurance the Government of India could not accept it in its entirety. No system of unemployment insurance was practicable in India. Because of the great size of the country and the comparative immobility of unskilled labor, the Government could not undertake any effective means for distributing public work to the unemployed in times of need as required by the fourth section of the recommendation.

---

[45] India, Council of State Debates, 1921, 1:165.
[46] Ibid.

In the Council of State, Lala Sukhbir Sinha, representing agricultural interests raised an objection to the establishment of employment agencies by the Government, on the ground that such a procedure would take laborers away from the rural districts to the manufacturing districts, and would thus be detrimental to agriculture.[47] It was, however, pointed out that employment agencies for Assam planters, Bengal jute millowners, and other interests, were already at work in rural districts. There was no reason, therefore, why the public agencies should not perform the same function with greater benefit to employers and employees alike.

In the consideration of the resolution regarding the desinfection of wool, it was pointed out that India needed such a provision for three reasons: First, for the protection of her own workers from anthrax diseases, especially as the tanning industry was growing rapidly and the source of danger was thus increasing. Second, India must consider her duty to other nations. Indian wool was responsible for some cases of anthrax in England. Third, India must protect her own industries. India herself prohibited the importation of various kinds of Japanese goods, such as brushes, as a precaution. Indian exporters of wool and wool products were liable to similar discriminations. Both chambers recommended, therefore, that the Governor General in Council should make an inquiry as to the possibility of arranging for the desinfection of wool and of providing disinfecting stations.

Industries giving rise to lead-poisoning among its workers were rather limited in India. Still, a resolution was passed prohibiting women and children from being employed in such industries.

The recommendation by the Washington Conference on health services, involved the establishment by each State, in addition to a system of efficient factory inspection, of a government service especially charged with the duties of safe-guarding the health of the workers. A resolution was moved by Sir Thomas Holland that the

[47] India, Council of States Debates, 1921, 1 : 169.

Government should examine the possibility of establishing the Government health service. An amendment was moved by Mr. Joshi recommending that the Government should establish such service instead of examining the possibility of giving effect to it. Most of the Assembly members supported the amendment. Munshi Iswar Saran favored a service "whose responsibility should be to look after the comforts and convenience of the workers and the sanitary conditions of the factories."[49] Mr. J. Chaudhuri suggested the appointment of woman physicians because women and children formed a large part of the labor population.[50]

Sir Thomas Holland stated that the Government had already been at work laying the foundation for carrying out the spirit of the recommendation. He pointed out, however, that the factory acts were administered by local governments and that the Legislative Assembly could not issue any orders to them. Promising that the Indian Government would recommend to the local governments the appointments of full-time medical men, also medical women for factory inspection, he asked for the withdrawal of the amendment, which being done, the original motion was carried.[51]

The hottest discussion took place, however, on the question of child labor. Resolutions were moved that the minimum age of children for admission into factories be raised from 9 years to 12. This was not to apply to factories employing more than 10 but less than 20 persons, unless the local governments so directed. Transitional regulations should be made regarding children between the ages of 9 and 12 already lawfully employed in factories.

The debate brought out the fact that the abolition of child labor was one of the important general principles enunciated in the last article of the labor section of the Peace Treaty. To this principle India had already sub-

---

48 Indian, Legislative Assembly Debates, 1921, 1:172.
49 Ibid., p. 278.
50 Ibid., p. 273.
51 Ibid., p. 279.

scribed that the privailing minimum age of 9 years was not only too low but led to considerable error. Owing to the lack of birth registration, the age certificate was determined by dentition and general physical development. It was found that even 7 or 8 year old children were passed as nine.[52] If the minimum age were raised to 12, this error might to a large extent be avoided. In favor of the 12 year minimum it was also pointed out that according to the Indian Penal Code, criminal liability did not exist before the age of 12 in any case, as before that age a child was considered unable to discriminate between right and wrong.

In the moving of the resolution, which was done by Mr. Chatterjee in the Council and Sir Thomas Holland in the Assembly, several arguments generally advanced against increasing the minimum age were criticized. In the first place, it was pointed out that the parents of children and the children themselves were opposed to such an increase. Mr. Chatterjee argued that this was only a personal opinion and could not very well be proven. On the other hand, even labor organizations demanded such an increase and they were supported in the demand by the press and the platform. In the second place, there was no advantage in raising the minimum age until educational facilities were provided for the children. Educational acts had been passed in some provinces, but they could not be carried out without funds. In refutation of this argument, it was maintained that as long as employers could employ under-aged children, they would never contribute to such funds. In the third place, raising the minimum age would result in considerable distress to many families which depended upon the earnings of children between 9 and 12. In reply to this argument, Mr. Chatterjee observed that there was something radically wrong with the wage system of a country where adult workers had to depend for the maintenance of their families upon the earnings of

---

[52] It is a practice among higher classes of the people to keep horoscopes which are a kind of unofficial birth registration.

children below the age of 12. Mr. Chatterjee reminded the members of the Council that in voting for the above resolution they should remember not only the children whose future would be affected by the decision and who had no special representatives in the Council, but also the well-being of many future generations in India.[53] In the fourth place, it was argued that such an increase in the minimum age of children would throw out a considerable amount of machinery adopted up to that time to children's use, especially in textile factories. In reply to this statement, Sir Thomas Holland remarked that there was a transitional period provided for in the resolution and in that time the factories ought to be able to adjust themselves to this gradual change.[54]

Sir Alexander Murray, President of the Jute Mills' Association, Calcutta, proposed an amendment in the council that the minimum age should be raised to 11 instead of 12. A similar amendment was brought forward by Sir L. P. Watson in the Legislative Assembly. There were several arguments advanced in favor of this amendment. Sir Alexander contended that the decision of the Government to raise the minimum age to 12 was influenced more by an anxiety to meet international obligations than by any material benefit likely to accrue to the children or to the country. He also maintained that the International Labor Conference imposed upon India the minimum of 12 years without due consideration of India's case. India ought to refuse adopting its resolution to show that the Conference had no right to do this. Moreover, Sir Alexander pointed out that the educational acts made provisions for only 4 years of schooling for children, and even if they attended school they would finish their education at about the age of 10 or 11. A minimum of 11 years would give an opportunity of going from school to the factory. Sir L. P. Watson observed that the boys in India between the ages of 9 and 14 exhibited an extraordinary intelligence and an adaptability to pick up their

[53] India, Council of State Debates, 1921, 1 : 177—78.

[54] India, Legislative Assembly Debates, 1921, 1 : 280—81.

work and to learn it quickly, which slowed down considerably after 14. An 11 year minimum would give a longer period of apprenticeship.[55]

Neither in the Assembly nor in the Council did the members favor the amendment. On the contrary, one member in the Council favored a minimum of 14 years and another in the Assembly proposed a minimum of even 15 years. The amendment was defeated.

Mr. Joshi proposed a second amendment making the new provision applicable to factories employing 10 persons. But Sir Thomas Holland objected to this amendment on the ground that it would be impossible for the Government to enforce such a provision without adequate provision for inspection. The amendment was withdrawn and the original motion was carried.[56]

Introduction of the Bill into the Legislature.

On March 1, 1921, a bill was at last introduced into the Legislative Assembly to amend the Factory Act of 1911.[57] The bill was based on the draft conventions and recommendations of the first International Labor Conference as ratified by the Indian Legislative Assembly and Council of State Minor changes were made in the light of a great mass of evidence collected through various commissions, committees, conferences, local governments, and various other official channels. The most important provisions of the bill were as follows:

First, the definition of the term factory was altered to include all establishments employing 20 or more persons and using mechanical power, and to empower local governments to extend the definition to establishments employing 10 persons or more, whether worked with mechanical power or not.

Second, a limitation of the weekly and daily maximum hours of work that could be worked in all factories, and an extension of the principles of limitation from the textile to all other factories.

---

[55] India, Council of State Debates, 1921, 1 : 182.
[56] India, Legislative Assembly Debates, 1921, 1 : 182.
[57] Ibid., p. 481—84.

Third, instead of half an hour ,all full time workers should, in the future, be granted an hour's rest after each six hours' work, and factory workers should ordinarily be entitled to a weekly day of rest which would preferably be Sunday.

Fourth, the minimum age of the employment of children was raised from 9 to 12, following the ratification by the Indian Government of the conventions and resolutions of the first International Labor Conference. There was also a further alteration, raising the upper age limit of children from 14 to 15.

Fifth, when a factory was speciallv and temporarily exempted by the local government from the operation of the 60 hour rule, the workers should be paid overtime at least 1¼ times the normal rate as required by the treaties with Germany and Austria.

On March 17 following, a motion was made by Sir Thomas Holland in the Legislative Assembly to refer the bill to a joint select committee of the Legislative Assembly and Council of State.[58] Since the introduction of the bill into the Assembly, some new features were added, the most important of which was the question of protecting the health and safety of the workers bv introducing, in addition to the regulations already in force, a further provision for controlling the artifical humidification of factories and for protecting the workers by placing on the employers the responsibility for ensuring the safety of factory buildings.

In seconding the motion, Mr. N. M. Joshi pointed out the anamoly in the definition of the factory, by which the Government of India gave local governments power to apply factory laws to establishments employing 10 persons and working with or without machinery, while not retaining the same power to itself. Mr. Joshi further pointed out that the safety and sanitary measures were not explicit enough for the guidance of factory inspectors, that there was no limit to which overtime work might extend, and that the penalties fixed for breach of law were very inadequate in certain cases.

[58] India, Legislative Assembly Debates, 1921, 1 : 1228—38.

Mr. A. B. Latthe proposed that there should be a provision in the bill to the effect that all children should have to produce certificate of attending school as a condition for admission to factory work.

With a few more suggestions, the resolution recommending the Council of State that the bill be referred to a joint select committee of both chambers was passed. On March 21, the Council of State passed a resolution to that effect,[59] and the Legislative Assembly referred the bill to a select committee on the same day.[60]

Passage of the Bill.

On January 10, 1922, a motion was made in the Legislative Assembly "that the report of the joint committee on the bill further to amend the Indian Factories Act, 1911, be taken into consideration."[61] It was pointed out at the outset that among the reasons for amending the existing law were the necessity of remedying the defects disclosed through ten years' experience and of adapting the provisions to the recent industrial advancement and to the growth of public opinion, and the fulfilment of international obligations.

Some of the provisions of the bill as introduced into the legislature were highly contentious. Three of the twelve members of the joint select committee each appended a minute of dissent, while three others also added a joint minute of dissent. Although there was unanimity of opinion on the main provisions, the amending bill underwent some important changes in the joint committee. The maximum number of hours in any one day was reduced from 12 to 11. It was also provided that every workman would secure 52 legal holidays in the year and that no worker would go without a holiday for more than ten days at a time.

Sir Vitaldas D. Thackersey, former member of the Factory Labor Commission of 1907, and representative of

---

[59] India, Council of State Debates, 1921, 1 : 520—23.
[60] India, Legislative Assembly Debates, 1921, 1 : 1460.
[61] Ibid., 1922, 2 : 1463—87.

Millowners' Association, raised several objections to the bill. He strongly criticised raising the maximum age of children from 14 to 15 on the following grounds: First, it went beyond the Washington convention or the law now in force in England, Japan and other countries, where, after the age of ten, boys and girls were allowed to work up to the maximum of 10 hours. Second, it was at the age of 15 that a boy was taken as an apprentice. The restriction on the half time work at that age would interfere with his employment and training. Third, a boy at 15 would not be satisfied with the half wages in factories while he could earn full wages outside. It would be especially harmful to a girl of 15, who, instead of working in the presence of her relatives in a factory, would work as a day laborer or a coolie away from them. Fourth, the innovation was introduced without consulting the laboring classes.

In reply to these objections, the following arguments were put forward by Mr. A. C. Chatterjee, Mr. Jamnadas Dwarkadas, and others. First, although young persons at 14 could work for 10 hours in England, yet no one before that age could be employed in factories. Second, life in India was so short and workers in Indian factories became incapable to continue work in factories so early that children should be given enough opportunity to grow into strong men and women and should not be made victims either of the ignorance of their parents or of the interests of the capitalists. Third, if the employers were so solicitous about depriving children of the means of livelihood, they could surely increase the wages in spite of the facts that they remained half-timers. Fourth, it was not true that the laboring classes would object to the provision. They have not done so in any of their numerous meetings. Moreover, the protection of women and children should not depend upon the consent of laborers or capitalists.

There were several other minor amendments brought forward in the Assembly, which were rejected after a short discussion. But the controversy centered around the amendment which provided that "if a child over the age of six years is found in any factory or within the precincts thereof, he shall, until the contrary is proved, be deemed to be employed in the factory."[62] In support of this provision, it was pointed out by the Government that there was a good deal of illegal employment of children in factories and without such strict regulation, the enforcement of the provisions regarding child labor would be impracticable. The opponents of this provision brought forward several arguments: First, it would put the burden of proof upon the employer, and under no system of jurisprudence did the burden of proof rest upon the accused person except in very exceptional cases. Second, there would be great hardship, if children were not allowed to attend mill schools, to play in the grounds, or to bring in food for their parents. After some controversy a provision was added to the effect that the premises used solely for purposes other than manufacturing processes, should not form part of the factory within the meaning of the law.

On the same day the resolution for the adoption of the bill as finally amended was passed.

On January 23 following, a motion was made in the Council of State for the adoption of the bill as passed by the Assembly, and, after some controversy, the bill was passed.[63] It comes into force on July 1 of the current year.

Chief Provisions of the Act.[64]

(1) A factory is any establishment employing not less than 20 persons and using mechanical power. A local government may define as factory any establishment employing not less than 10 persons and working with or without mechanical power.

The distinction between textile and non-textile factories was abolished as far as the law was concerned. The

[62] India, Legislative Assembly Debates, 1922, 2 : 1476.
[63] India, Council of State Debates, 1922, 2 : 649—59.
[64] The Commerce, Calcutta, Jan. 21, 1922, p. 110; the Times Trade Supplement, London, April 8, 1922, p. 65, and Labor Gazette, Bombay, March, 1922, pp. 27—30.

scope of the provisions by which a large number of factories was exempted from the operation of the act was limited.

(2) The minimum age for the employment of children was raised from 9 to 12 and the maximum age from 14 to 15. The hours of work of children were limited to 6 in any one day. No child can be employed without medical certificate, and a child may be re-examined for the continuance of his work, if necessary.

(3) No adult should work more than 11 hours in any one day, nor more than 60 hours in any one week.

(4) All workers should have a period of one hour's rest for work exceeding 6 hours. At the option of workers, this period might be divided into two.

(5) All workers should have a day of rest in a week and no worker should go without a holiday for more than 10 days at a time.

(6) In case of over-time work, workers should receive at least 1¼ times the normal rate.

(7) The fine for the breach of the act is raised from Rs. 200 to Rs. 500, and the court is given power to pay compensation to injured persons and their families out of the fine.

(8) Prohibition of the employment of women and young persons under 18 in certain lead processes.

(9) The Governor General in Council was empowered to make rules for the disinfection of wool infected with anthrax.

CHAPTER VI.

ADMINISTRATION OF THE LAW.

An equitable law always implies an adequate provision for its administration. Even a good law is worse than no law unless it is enforced. In order to have a proper understanding of the factory law it is, therefore, essential to see what means have been provided for its administration.

Administrative Organisation.

The administration of the factory law is intimately connected with the general administration of a country, which in India falls into three principal divisions:[1]

First, the Home Government with the Secretary of State for India, who is a member of the British Cabinet, and of the India Council in England. This council is divided into committees. The committee concerned with Indian factories is that of revenue and statistics, especially the division of statistics.

Second, the Government of India, with a Governor General, and an executive council and legislature, the latter consisting of the Council of State and the Legislative Assembly. The executive council is divided into departments which, in turn, are subdivided into divisions. The departments which have immediate relations with the administration of factories are: In the first place, the home department, especially the divisions of health, the police, the judiciary, the municipality, and the local board. In the second place, the department of commerce and industries, which was created in 1907 with a division of factory administration. Recently the Government of India has also establshed, in connection with the Board of Industries and Munitions, a Central Labor Bureau, for the collection and distribution of information and for advice to the local governments as well as to employers and employees.

[1] Since this writing, there have been some notable changes in the constitution of the Home as well as the India Government.

Third, the provincial or local governments, with generally a governor and executive and legislative councils. The administration of local governments is divided into several departments on practically the same basis as that of the India Government. Every local government is divided into a number of districts with an officer, called variously in different parts of the country, magistrate, collector, collector-magistrate and deputy commissioner. Two or more districts may be joined together into a division under the administration of an officer called commissioner.

A district is the unit of political organization in India. The magistrate-collector is the chief executive officer, and virtually the supreme authority in the district. A district is generally subdivided into smaller divisions with respective officers, who are directly under the supervision of the district collector. Beside the executive function, the magistrate-collector also administers justice in all criminal cases. The administration of justice in civil suits is left to especially appointed judegs of whom there is at least one in each district. The district judiciary whether of the criminal or civil court, is responsible to the High or Chief Court, located at the metropolis of each local government. Appeal from the latter court may be made in certain cases to the Privy Council in England.

Several territories are directly under the jurisdiction of the India Government. Besides, there are native states which have certain freedom in local affaires.

A scheme of the constitution of the Government of India is shown in the diagram on p. 166.

In the case of Bombay and other local governments, it is the general department, corresponding to the home department of the India Government, which is in charge of factory affairs. Until the year 1912 the magistrate was the ex-officio inspector of factories in all districts, except in metropolitan cities like Calcutta, where other officials were in direct charge. Even the work of special technical inspectors was carried on under his supervision. By the Factory Act of 1911 this power was largely given over to special inspectors, e. g., chief inspector of fac-

The Government of India.

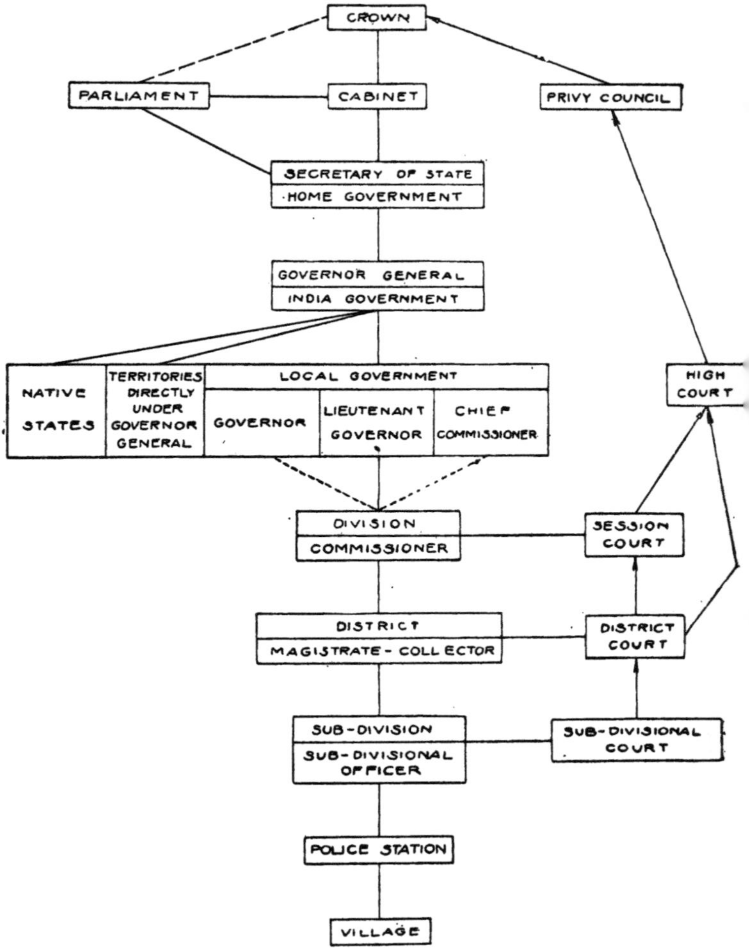

tories in Bombay. But in certain provinces, e. g., the Central Provinces and Berar, the power to prosecute cases has been reserved to the magistrate.

In February, 1920, a Commissioner of Labor was appointed by the Government of Madras, whose duties included the supervision of factory inspection and of the immigration of labor. His field of activity embraces practically all economic aspects of labor, including the organization of labor, cooperative housing, and the health and welfare of labor in general. Bombay has established a similar office.

Enactment and Modification.

The supreme authority regarding factory legislation, as in fact regarding all legislation in India, rests with the Indian Legislature. The acts passed are general, compulsory for the whole of India, and uniform in their essential features. Local governments cannot undertake the enactment of factory laws, which may, by the regulation of working hours and other conditions, result in the restriction of trade; but before the enforcement of the laws enacted by the Central Government, they can, through certain powers granted by the provisions of the acts themselves, undertake modifications in minor details to suit their own special needs. Such procedure on the part of the local governments has been necessitated by the great diversity in the nature of the industries and in the geographical and meteorological conditions in the different sections of the country.

This power of modification was granted to the local governments under Sections 9, 13, and 18, of the Factory Act of 1891. Under Section 9, for instance, a local government might direct the occupier[2] or manager of a factory to register all children in such form and in such particulars as the local government might from time to time designate. Under Section 13, the manager must give

[2] Occupier means the manager and includes any person for the time being actually in charge of a factory. Notification by the Government of Bengal. Gt. Brit. Parl. Papers, 1893-94, Vol. 65, H. of C. 151, p. 4.

notice of an accident to the designated authorities. And under Section 18, the local government was empowered to make rules consistent with the act and subject to the control of the Governor General in Council. These rules might provide for fencing of machinery and mill-gearing, maintenance of water supply, ventilation, cleanliness and prohibition of overcrowding. But even in these matters a certain degree of uniformity was attained through a system by which all local governments were required to make report on certain definite points, such as: —

(1) A summary of results and a general resumé of inspections.

(2) Sanitary conditions and arrangements in factories.

(3) General health of operatives, especially of women and children.

(4) Wages and general conditions of operatives; a general information only.

(5) Employment of women and children and an account of the work of certifying surgeons.

(6) Fencing of machinery and mill-gearing.

(7) Convictions should be entered in the prescribed statement and detailed accounts given in the body of the report.

The Government of Bombay, for example, made several rules and orders on June 22, 1892, i. e., a few days before the second factory act came into force, which were called the Bombay Factory Rules of 1892. The words and expressions in these rules and orders were interpreted to have the same force as if they were embodied in the act. Under these rules, each factory was to supply two gallons of water for each employee per day; to provide an area of 36 superficial feet and a breathing area of 500 cubic feet with 10 square feet of ventilating openings for each employee in the room to prevent inhalation of injurious dust, if any; to lime-wash the walls and ceiling every fourteen months, to provide one latrine for every 50 employees, and so on.[3] It also provided: —

---

[3] Gt. Brit. Parl. Papers, 1893—94, Vol. 65, H. of C. 151, pp. 22—24.

(1) That an inspector[4] should visit each factory at least once in every three months.

(2) That every order given by the inspector to the occupier of a factory should be in writing with his signature.

(3) That the occupier might make appeal against any order of the inspector, if necessary.

(4) That the inspector should make a report of all his work within a certain period.

(5) That the occupier of every factory, in which children were employed, should keep, in a form prescribed by the Government, a register of the children employed and of their respective employments.

(6) That the occupier should send notice of accidents, if any, to the inspector, or the magistrate, or any other officer designated, within one hour in case of death, within 12 hours in case of fatal injury and within 48 hours in case of minor injury.

The Government of Bengal made similar rules under the Act of 1891. Unlike the Government of Bombay, the Bengal Government did not make any specific rules regarding the supply of water, air space, etc. Each factory was to be inspected only once in every 6 months, the inspector to keep a register of the factories inspected and of the accidents reported in his jurisdiction.

The occupier must keep a muster roll of the children employed and a register of the hours worked.[5]

The rules made by other local governments were practically the same in nature, though they differed in details.[6]

After necessary modification, the law is left to inspectors or other especially appointed officers for execution.

---

[4] Inspector means the magistrate of the district or a special inspector. — Notification by the Government of Bengal. Gt. Brit. Parl. Papers, 1893—94, Vol. 65, H. of C. 151, p. 4.

[5] Ibid., pp. 4—6.

[6] Ibid., pp. 10—12.

Inspection and Supervision.

The most important branch of factory administration is inspection. It is both interesting and significant to note how the system of factory inspection has developed in India in a comparatively short period of time.

Under the factory act of 1881, the local governments were empowered either to appoint special factory inspectors or to entrust the work of inspection to magistrates or some other officers. In 1883 the Government of Bombay appointed a special inspector, but the position was abolished in 1887.[7] The other local governments made over the work to district magistrates, who were *ex-officio* inspectors, the magistrates in turn often delegated their work to their subordinates or other officials.

In 1889, in reply to an inquiry by the Secretary of State regarding the efficiency of inspection by ex-officio inspectors, the Governor General stated that the opinion of all the local governments and administrations was favorable to the maintenance of the system of inspection by district magistrates.[8]. The subject was also discussed by the Factory Commission of 1890. The arguments put forward by the adherents of the system of inspection by *ex-officio* inspectors, were: — First, the factories were small in number and scattered over a vast area. The inspection by special agents would be, therefore, costly. Second, such inspection would also be inefficient, as the approach of the special inspector to the locality would always be known beforehand. On the other hand, the magistrate was always on the spot and could make a surprise visit at any time. Third, the lack of technical knowledge on the part of such inspectors might be met by appointing a few boiler inspectors, such as locomotive superintendents of railroads or their subordinates, who might be paid from fees.[9] For the rest of the work, the education and intelligence of a magistrate or of any other high official were sufficient.

---

[7] Imperial Gazetteer of India, 1907, 3 : 257.
[8] Gt. Brit. Parl. Papers, 1889, Vol. 58, H. of C. 162, p. 3.
[9] *Ibid.*, 1894, Vol. 58, H. of C. 108, p. 133.

Whatever might have been the merits or demerits of these arguments, no attempt was made by any local government to appoint any special inspector until 1892, when two such inspectors were appointed, one for the Bombay Presidency and the Central Provinces and another for the Bengal Presidency and the United Provinces.[10] Even the system of inspection by *ex-officio* inspectors was not uniform. The chief inspector of factories in the city of Bombay in 1905, for example, was the Assistant Collector of Bombay. The duty of medical inspection was entrusted to the personal assistant of the surgeon general and that of certification of age to three Presidency surgeons. In the Presidency, outside the city of Bombay, factory inspection was carried on by collectors, assistant and deputy collectors, and the special inspector. In Calcutta, the chief inspector was the commissioner of police to whom the special inspectors had to report. In the city of Madras, both special and medical inspectors had to report to the sanitary engineer of the Government; and in the Presidency of Madras, the work of inspection was given over to civil servants. In the Punjab, inspection was made by the deputy commissioner[11] or by some other officers deputed by him; in the United Provinces, by civil surgeons, district officers, and the special inspector from Calcutta; and in the Central Provinces by the deputy commissioners, civil surgeons, and the special inspector from Bombay.[12] Under these circumstances, the Textile Factory Labor Committee of 1906 strongly recommended the appointment of special inspectors of factories, having in mind both the efficiency of the work and the preservation of the uniformity of the law. The Factory Labor Commission of 1907 also took up the matter and recommended discontinuing the system of appointing *ex-officio* inspectors and placing the special inspectors under the direct control of some district officials, as in Bombay.

---

[10] Imperial Gazetteer of India, 1907, 3 : 247.

[11] Same as magistrate and collector in Bengal and some other provinces.

[12] Gt. Brit. Parl. Papers, 1907, Vol. 59, Cd. 3617, p. 9.

Meanwhile the importance of appointing special inspectors in order to secure efficiency in work was realized by several local governments and the number of such inspectors throughout the country was raised to 6 in 1908. They were distributed as follows: — Bombay 3, Madras 1, the Central Provinces 1, and Bengal and the United Provinces 1. The Factory Act of 1911, which came into force on July 1, 1912, made special provision for the appointment of special factory inspectors and on March 31, 1913, there were 14 such inspectors in the country, five of them being in the Presidency of Bombay alone. Besides these special inspectors, there were also boiler inspectors and certifying surgeons in each district.[13] In the city of Bombay including the district of Thana, a whole-time officer was appointed on July 7, 1912, for the certification of children. In the other districts throughout the Presidency of Bombay, the work was carried on by medical officers, appointed by the Bombay Government.[14] District magistrates are still retained as ex-officio inspectors, but their duty is generally confined to ascertaining that the orders issued by inspectors are observed.[15]

One of the points of discussion before the Factory Commission of 1907 related to the recruiting of factory inspectors. It will be remembered that experience in India and the ability to converse with the employees in their own language were, according to the commission, the essential qualifications for the posts of inspectors. The commission supported the view of the Bombay Government that recruitment of factory inspectors from the United Kingdom was not necessary. Such recruits would be entirely ignorant of local conditions and requirements and might cause embarassment by attempting to introduce measures not suited to Indian conditions. There was nothing, argued the commission, in the work

---

[13] Gt. Brit. Parl. Papers, 1914, Vol. 63, H. of C. 288, p. 65.

[14] Bombay Presidency Factory Department. Annual Report 1912, Bombay, 1913, p. 4.

[15] Gt. Brit. Parliamentary Debates, H. of C, 39 : 1191.

of inspectors to justify their being sent to Europe for training.[16]

In reply to an inquiry as to whether all the factory inspectors in India should be Europeans, the Under Secretary of State for India in the House of Commons said, on June 13, 1912, that as the great majority of the managers and their assistants in Indian factories were Europeans, it was inevitable that the inspecting staff should be mainly, if not wholly, made up of Europeans.[17] On November 26, 1912, Mr. Jowett asked the Under Secretary of State for India in the House of Commons whether, since out of 2,430 factory managers, some 2000 or 82 per cent were Indians and almost all factory employees were Indians, the Under Secretary should not take steps to appoint an adequate number of Indian factory inspectors. Indian factory inspectors were acquainted with the conditions prevailing in factories and spoke the same language as employees did, and would, therefore, perform better service. The Under Secretary replied that European managers were employed in the larger factories and the first hand knowledge of the working of the factory act in England was an important qualification.[18] When the appointments were made, all of the 14 inspectors were found to be Europeans, or British strictly speaking, but only 4 of them were appointed in England, 2 of these having had experience in factories and the other 2 having qualified themselves for the factory inspection staff in England. The other 10 were appointed in India and had had no experience in factories or in business.[19]

Some idea of the coordination and interrelation of the different departments of the Government, as far as factory administration is concerned, may be formed from the following review and diagram on p. 174.

---

[16] Gt. Brit. Parl. Papers, 1909, Vol. 63, Cd. 4519, p. 38.

[17] Gt. Brit. Parliamentary Debates, H. of C., 1912, 39 : 1191.

[18] Ibid., 44 : 987.

[19] Ibid., 1914, 60 : 1163.

Factory Administration in India.

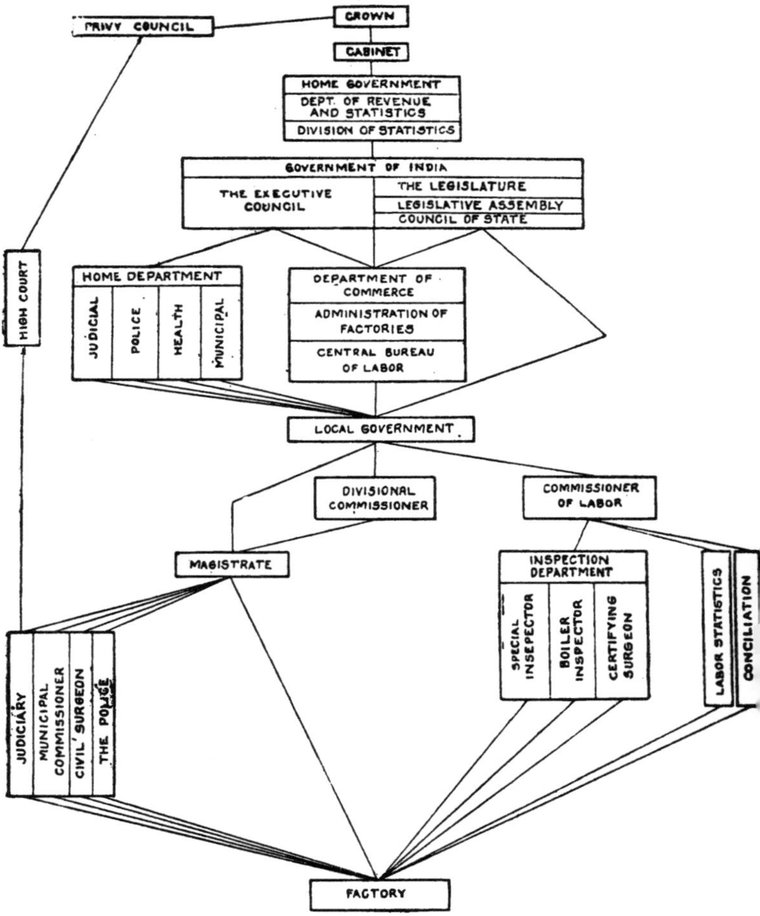

Suppose a capitalist desires to start a factory in the City of Bombay. He applies first to the commissioner of municipality[20] for plans and directions, by following which he can fulfil the requirements of safety and sanitation in his intended plant. After the establishment of his plant, he notifies the chief inspector of factories,[21] who is the head of the inspecting staff in the City of Bombay; and in response the boiler inspector inspects the boilers and the certifying surgeon examines the children and issues certificates of age and physical fitness for employment. The special inspector examines the whole plant, including safety, sanitation, employement of women, children and men, and number of hours to be worked, and gives orders, if necessary, to remedy any shortcoming before the commencement of work. So the business starts.

Suppose now an accident happens. If it is serious, the manager of the factory at once sends the injured person to a hospital and at the same time informs the police and the special inspector of the accident. The inspector investigates the nature and cause of the injury, and is assisted in his inquiry by the police and the civil surgeon under whose supervision the injured person is treated. If the inspector finds that the accident has occurred because of neglect of duty on the part of the manager, he brings a suit against him in the court of the magistrate, he himself being the prosecuter. If convicted, the manager has the option of appeal to higher courts.

Special inspectors report on their work to the chief inspector of factories, who at the end of the year sends a formal report with some observations, if necessary, to the General Department of the Bombay Government. The Bombay Government sends all such reports with additional observations to the Division of Factory Administration of the Department of Commerce and Industry, and the latter department issues a general annual report which is embodied in the other reports of the Government of

[20] Gt. Brit. Parl. Papers, 1888, H. of C. 321, 77 : 20.

[21] Bombay Presidency Factory Dept. Annual Report, 1912, Bombay 1912, p. 3.

India. Finally, a summarized report, with some observations of the Government of India, is published every year by the India Office in England and included in Parliamentary papers.

Penalties and Prosecutions.

The enforcement of law implies that there are penalties in case it is not complied with. The enactment of a legislative measure is thus always accompanied by provision for specific penalties in case of violation. The Factory Act of 1891, for example, provided penalties for any one, who employed children in dangerous work, e. g., cleaning mill-gearing, while the machinery was in motion, or neglected any of the following rules: — (1) Keeping of a prescribed register for children. (2) Setting up of notices of danger in proper places. (3) Fencing of machinery or mill-gear. (4) Supply of a required amount of water per employee. (5) Provision for proper ventilation as prescribed by the inspector. (6) Provision for necessary and prescribed space per worker. (7) Sending of notices of, or furnishing of reports on accidents, etc. The penalty for any of these offences was a fine of 200 rupees, provided the prosecution was instituted by the permission of the inspector in charge of the factory concerned. There was also a fine of 20 rupees for the offense of using, or helping others use, a false certificate of the age of children.

Conflicting opinions exist regarding the observation of the law by factories. The reports on the working of the Factory Act of 1881 seemed to indicate that the principle provisions of the law were well observed all over the country.[22] The reports on the working of the Factory Act of 1891 led practically to the same conclusion.[23] The violation of the law generally occurred in the case of the employment of children. The Factory Commission of 1890 found several half-timers employed as full-timers.[24] On the other hand, the Madras Government did not believe

[22] Gt. Brit. Parl. Papers, 1889, Vol. 58, H. of C. 124, pp. 3, 34, 48.
[23] Ibid., Vol. 58, H. of C. 108, p. 48.
[24] Ibid., 1890—91, Vol. 59, H. of C. 86, p. 110.

that the evasion of the law regarding the employment of children below the age of 9 years was frequent.[25] "In connection with certain restrictions", wrote the collector of land revenue, in charge of Bombay factory inspection, "such as the long midday rest for women and the reduced hours for children, as the workers would gladly be free of these restrictions, irregularities are difficult of detection and may occur. At the same time, if such irregularities occur, they are not common."[26] The opinion of the Government of the Central Provinces on July 31, 1893, was of the same tenor. "The inspection reports of the special inspector and of the civil surgeon show," observed the government, "that the provision of the factories act and of the rules framed thereunder were, in the main, faithfully observed by occupiers of factories."[27]

During the recent years, the reports regarding the observation of child labor law have been conflicting. "My experience of one year as medical inspector in Bombay," wrote the medical officer in charge of the Bombay factories in 1906, "leads me to believe that the existing law as to the employment of children is not evaded, nor do I think that mill managers have any desire to evade the law, nor anything to gain by doing so."[28] This might have been only a casual remark, as the officer's experience in factory inspection was limited to one year. But the report of the government, issued just a year previous to the above statement, made substantially the same observation. "As in the previous years," continued the report, "there are but few instances reported of the infringement of these provisions of the act, which relate to the working hours and employment of women and children."[29] Yet according to the report of 1912, it was found that no law was so much violated as the child labor law. Many children under false name took double certificates. While the average number of children employed

[25] Gt. Brit. Parl. Papers, 1894, Vol. 58, H. of C. 108, p. 49.
[26] Ibid., p. 53.
[27] Ibid., p. 168.
[28] Ibid., 1909, Vol. 63, Cd. 4519, p. 57.
[29] Ibid., 1908, Vol. 75, H. of C. 145, p. 176.

in Bombay was 4,300, some 13,000 passes were issued to children of that city every year.[30] Practically the same observation has been made by inspectors of factories in the recent years.

A fair estimate of the obsrvance of the factory law may be had from the number of persons convicted for the breach of the act. It is not to be assumed that the convictions actually represent the number of cases in which the law is violated. In many cases, the prosecution does not take place for lack of proper inspection and, if it does, the technical difficulties often absolve the violator. A rough idea nevertheless may be formed from the statistics of conviction for the violation of the factory act.

The statistics prior to the year 1892 are not available. In that year 6 persons were convicted for breach of the factory law. The number of convictions fell to 3 in 1898, but rose to 37 in 1903. In 1914 there were 162 convictions in all parts of the country, but in 1917 only 154 were recorded.[31] The convictions were made for such offenses as irregular employment of women and children and the failure to send in prescribed returns.[32]

The provisions of the Factory Act of 1911 were extended to include all factories employing 50 persons or upward, and might by order of any local government be further extended to factories employing 20 persons. Although only two provinces exercised this power, many seasonal establishments were thus brought under the operation of the law, and the additional inspections provided by it have made possible a better and more elaborate system of inspection. The factory act of 1922 has gone still farther and empowered the local governments to include establishments employing 10 persons and working with or without power.

---

[30] Bombay Factory Report, 1913, p. 1. See also Punjab, Hyderabad, and C. P. & Berar Factory Reports.

[31] Statistical abstract relating to British India, London, 1920, p. 235.

[32] Gt. Brit. Parl. Papers, 1917, H. of C. 136, p. 27.

CHAPTER VII.

SUMMARY AND CONCLUSIONS.

Th Act of 1881.

The rapid progress made in the cotton industry in India soon after the establishment of the steam power factory in the City of Bombay in 1863, gave rise to a spirit of rivalry among Lancashire manufacturers, who, becoming apprehensive of losing their trade with India, which consisted of about one-fourth of their annual export, started strong agitation with a twofold object in view: First, to free the Indian market from the import duty on cotton goods. Second, to bring the factories in India under the same regulations as those in England. In 1874, a deputation of the Manchester Chamber of Commerce waited upon Lord Salisbury, then the Secretary of State for India, to urge upon him the regulation of factory labor in India. Shortly after, Lord Salisbury advised the Government of India to repeal the import duty on cotton goods and recommended the subject of factory legislation to the consideration of the Government of Bombay.

The demand of the Secretary of State upon the Government of India to repeal a revenue duty in order to please Manchester interests, was strongly criticized both in England and India. Fiscal difficulties, however, did not permit the Government of India to repeal the import duty on cotton goods, but the Manchester agitation in Parliament, nevertheless succeeded in passing, in 1877, a resolution to the effect that the import duty on cotton goods should be repealed by the Government of India at the earliest opportunity.

In the meantime, the Government of Bombay appointed, in 1875, a commission to inquire into the conditions of factories and to report on the advisability of enacting laws for the regulation of child and woman labor. The majority of the commission, however, failed to see the necessity for such regulation and the Government of Bombay refused to take any further action.

The refusal of the Government of Bombay to regulate factory labor in India revived the Manchester agitation. While the public in India resented the attempt of the Manchester interests to interfere with India's internal affairs, the manufacturing interests being apprehensive lest the cotton industry, in which they had invested large sums of money, be strangled in its infancy, started a counter-agitation to thwart the designs of the Manchester interests. Meanwhile, philanthropists also instituted a movement in India for the betterment of factory conditions by legislative regulation, and appealed both to Manchester interests and to British philanthropists for help. As a result, a resolution was moved in Parliament in 1879 praying Her Majesty for the immediate regulation of child and woman labor in Indian factories.

In the same year the Government of India introduced a bill for factory regulation. The first factory act was enacted in 1881 and the law became operative on July 1 of that year. The most important provisions of the act were the fixing of the minimum and maximum age limits for the employment of children at 7 and 12 years respectively, and the limitation of their working hours to 9 in any one day.

The Act of 1891.

The very year the first factory act was passed, Lancashire manufacturers sustained a still further loss of their trade with India and sent a deputation to the Secretary of State for India to urge the repeal of the duty on their goods imported into India. In 1882 this duty was completely abolished. The first object of their agitation was thus won by the Manchester interests.

The provisions of the factory act, however, failed to satisfy the demands of both the philanthropists and the Manchester interests, and no sooner was the act enacted than agitation was started again to amend it. In 1882 a Manchester factory inspector investigated conditions prevailing in Bombay factories and made some suggestions for improvement. In 1884, the Government of Bombay appointed a commission to consider these suggestions in all their bearings. Meanwhile, the factory workers of Bombay held their first conference and sent a memorandum to the commission for the redress of their grievances. The commission made several recommendations which were sent to the Government of India, but the latter declined to take any action. In 1887, another inspector of British factories made a similar investigation in Bombay and on his return to England, made several allegations against the factories in India. In 1888, the Secretary of State for India directed that these charges be considered by the Government of India.

In the meantime, the cotton industry in India was making still more rapid progress, and the spirit of rivalry among the Lancashire manufacturers was again aroused. In 1888, the Manchester Chamber of Commerce passed a resolution recommending the extension of the British child and woman labor laws to India, and soon after sent a deputation to the Secretary of State for India to present this resolution. Such attempts on the part of the Manchester interests created resentment and apprehension among the Indian public, especially among cotton manufacturers.

In reply to the inquiry of the Secretary of State, the Government of India denied the charges made by the British factory inspector, but consented to amend the factory act according to the recommendation of the Bombay Factory Commission of 1884, and accordingly introduced a bill into the Legislative Council. Under the pressure of the Manchester interests, the Secretary of State insisted on stricter measures and the Government of India postponed the passage of the bill.

The delay in the amendment of the factory act by the Government of India led to fresh agitation in England. An attempt was forthwith made to apply to India some of the resolutions of the International Labor Conference of Berlin held in 1890. A demand was also made that the Government of India should submit a draft of the bill to the British Parliament before its passage by the Indian Legislative Council, although such a procedure was against the constitutional right of the Government of India.

During this agitation in Great Britain, India was not free from similar demonstrations, the most important of which was agitation among the workers themselves, who founded an organisation of their own called the Millhands' Association of Bombay and held a great mass meeting at which they drew up a memorandum of their demands.

On the advice of the Secretary of State, the Government of India appointed a commission to inquire into the conditions of factory workers. The commission received an address from the Millhands' Association and, after due investigation, recommended increasing the age limits of children in industry and regulating the working hours of women. But the Manchester interests did not find the recommendations restrictive enough and influenced the Secretary of State to demand for stricter regulation. The Government of India made several concessions, though under protest, and submitted the bill into the legislature for final decision. It was passed in 1891, and came into force on January 1, 1892. The chief provision of the act was the regulation of woman labor to 11 hours as resolved by the Berlin labor conference, with an interval of rest for an hour and a half.

The Act of 1911.

No sooner was the Factory Act of 1891 passed than agitation was started in England to amend it. An inquiry into factory conditions undertaken by the Government of India in 1892 at the request of the British Royal Commission on Labor revealed the fact that the interests of both labor and capital were not adequately served by the provisions of the new act.

About this time, the rapid progress of the jute industry in Bengal aroused the rival spirit of the Dundee Chamber of Commerce which passed resolutions in 1894 advocating stricter factory legislation for India. The agitation of the jute interests in Great Britain was highly resented by British capitalists who invested money in the jute industry of India.

In the meantime, great changes were taking place in the cotton industry. Following the enactment of the factory act of 1891, the industry met one misfortune after another. On the other hand, the fiscal difficulties early in the ninetees led the Government of India to levy a revenue duty on all imported goods including cotton manufactures. But in order to satisfy the Manchester interests, the Government of India was obliged to levy a countervailing excise duty of 3.5 per cent on all Indian cotton manufactures which in any way competed with Lancashire cotton goods. In 1904—05 the cotton industry in India underwent, however, a complete change. The low price of cotton and the profitable market both at home and abroad led to unusual activities in factories which were soon followed by excessive hours of work. The investigation of factory conditions by the Government in 1905, revealed the fact that out of 74 mills inspected, 16 mills worked 14 hours or more a day and 33 mills about 13 hours or more. The Bombay factory workers also sent a memorandum to the Government of India praying for the regulation of their working hours by legislation. The question of factory legislation was, therefore, reopened by the Government of India and a bill was introduced into the Legislative Council in 1905.

In the meantime, the Bengalees boycotted all British goods as a protest against the partition of Bengal by the Government of India. The boycott was soon followed by Swadeshi, or the use of domestic goods, and many handicraft industries were revived; and even a new cotton factory was started by the leaders of the movement. Considerable apprehension was, therefore, felt by the Lancashire manufacturers, who sold to Bengal more than one-half of their export to India. A deputation of the Factory Workers' Association of Lancashire waited upon the Secretary of State for India in 1906 to demand restrictions on the labor of adult males in Indian factories.

In the same year, the Government of India appointed a committee to inquire into the conditions of textile factories. This committee was followed in 1907 by a commission which investigated into the conditions of factories of all kinds in India. Both the committee and the commission advocated the regulation of adult male labor in textile factories, but the latter was strongly opposed to direct legislation for the purpose.

A new bill was introduced in 1909 and passed in 1911. The act became effective on January 1, 1912. The chief provision of the act was the limitation of working hours of male laborers to 12 hours a day and of children to 6 hours in textile factories.

The Act of 1922.

Not long after the enactment of the third factory act, the world was plunged into the Great War in which India had to take an active part on the side of the Allies. As in other countries, the war brought about great political and industrial changes in India. The national party, started in 1905 as a protest against the partition of Bengal, became a powerful body which aimed at the establishment of Swaraj, or national government. There was recently established a new constitution, which, while not giving the people any practical control of the government of the country, nevertheless created a much better means for the expression of public opinion on national questions. There appeared an intelligent public which was quite alive to its rights and interests. A new background for the enactment of factory legislation in India was thus created.

The textile industries which were making only a fair profit before the war, entered into a period of unprecedented expansion during its progress. Some new industries, such as those related to hides and skins and oilseeds, made their start. This industrial development was accompanied by a change in the industrial policy of the Government, which, on May 19, 1916, appointed a commission to report on the possibility of further industrial progress. On the other hand, a well-organized capitalistic class appeared among the Indians themselves.

The war put a heavy financial burden upon India. She had not only to finance the campaigns she undertook herself, but she made a gift of £ 100,000,000 to Great Britain towards the cost of the war. As a consequence, it became necessary for India to reform her tariff and raise her import duties. The duties on cotton goods imported from Lancashire were raised from 3½ to 7½ per cent, while the countervailing excise duty of 3½ per cent on cotton manufactured in India was left untouched. The Lancashire manufacturers raised a strong protest and sent a deputation urging His Majesty's Government to revoke the decision of the Government of India. In this they were unsuccessful. This defeat of the Manchester interests in controlling the import duties of India was followed by another defeat in their attempt at interfering with Indian factory legislation.

The Great War at last came to a close and an international labor organization consisting of an international labor office and a general conference of representatives of the members was created under the auspices of the League of Nations of the Peace Treaty. The conference held its first meeting at Washington, D. C., in 1919 and drew up draft conventions and recommendations for the amelioration of labor conditions in countries subscribing to the League. India was asked, among other things, to reduce the working hours in factories from 72 to 60 a week and to raise the minimum age of children from 9 to 12 years.

In the meantime, a new force appeared in India. The labor movement which had started in 1875 appeared as one of the strongest organisations in 1919—20. Through successive strikes, it paralysed the industrial organisation of the whole country, realised some of its immediate aims and even won the sympathy of the public and the recognition of the Government.

At first the Government of India was not in favor of the ratification of the conventions and recommendations of the First International Labor Conference. But the ratification was strongly urged by the British Parliament, the Indian public, and the subsequent International Labor Conference. With some modifications, the Government of India at last ratified them.

Soon after, a bill based mostly on the recommendations of the Industrial Commission and on the conventions and recommendations of the International Labor Conference as ratified by the Government, was introduced into the legislature and referred to a joint select committee of the Legislative Assembly and the Council of State. On January 10, 1922, the report of the joint committee was taken up by the Legislative Assemblv for final consideration, and the bill, after a few minor amendments, was passed. On January 23, the bill, as amended and passed by the Legislative Assembly, was also passed by the Council of State.

The essential features of the act were the extension of the scope of the factory law to smaller establishments, the increase in the minimum and maximum age limits of factory children to 12 and 15 respectively and the limitation of the daily and weekly working hours of adults to 11 and 60 respectively.

Concluding Remarks.

One of the fundamental conceptions of the eighteenth century philosophy was the theory of the divine ordinance of nature. Emanating from this ordinance, man was a rational being, who knew what was the best for himself and who, by following his own interest, promoted the welfare of the whole society. Every individual had certain natural and inalienable rights, such as private property, free competition and freedom of contract, upon the maintenance of which depended the harmony of social interests. The main function of government, according to this theory, was the preservation of these individual rights.

When the factory system made its appearance and brought about the industrial revolution, the doctrines of laissez faire and individualism thus pervaded the social mind. Private initiative and enterprise, which were repressed by the State in the mercantilistic period, received new impetus. Profit-making became the prime incentive in business organisation. Capitalism took its rise and inaugurated modern industrialism. The factory system made a very rapid progress leading to the phenomenal growth of social capital, which increased national dividend and more or less benefited all classes of people. But it was not long before self-interest asserted itself among the capitalists and led them to the exploitation of the laboring classes, especially women and children. Children of tender age were worked day and night and often the same number of hours as adults. It was the "bitter cry" of children, many of whom were the wards of the State, which led the British Government to enact the child labor law and to lay the foundation of factory legislation.

Since the enactment of the first factory act over a century ago, there has been great modification in social thoughts. The classical doctrines upon which were based the political and economic theories of the last century have undergone radical changes. Individual rights have often been found detrimental to social welfare. There has gradually grown up a social consciousness which places social interests above those of individuals and classes. Government has become a means for the promotion of public welfare such as health, education and morals. The protective power of the State has been extended to men and women working in modern industries, such as mines and factories. Factory legislation has thus become an important political institution.

The factory system has evolved through the gradual conquest of nature by man and is the most efficient method of production known up to the present time. While the remedy of the defects which are still inherent in its process and the control of the abuses which may prevail in its operation are the chief objects of factory legislation, it also aims so to direct the normal growth of the factory system that the latter may become the most economic means for the utilisation of natural resources and for the augmentation of national wealth. The inequality in the present system of distribution, such as low wages and unemployment, largely arise from the capitalistic control of industry rather than from the factory system. They are more or less common to all classes of laborers working under the wage system. The solution of these problems depends upon the democratisation of the present industrial organisation rather than upon factory legislation.

The problems of factory legislation proper relate chiefly to such questions as excessive hours, sickness and accidents, compensation and insurance, and child and woman labor. The remedial measures are, however, beset with several difficulties: First, lack of knowledge regarding prevention and remedy in many cases. Second, inertia of human nature not to be prompt to take advantage of the protective devices even when they are known. Third, doctrines of natural rights under the notion of which some people still oppose social legislation. Fourth, reluctance and resistance on the part of capitalistic interests to introduce any method or to accept any measure which enchroaches upon their vested rights or reduces their profit. The solution of the problems lies in overcoming these difficulties by education in modern science and philosophy and in introducing progressive legislation as determined by the enlightened public and the organised workers.

Factory legislation in India, while following the same process of growth and meeting the same kind of difficulties as in other countries, presents some additional problems. The extreme poverty of the people and the primitive nature of the industries make the rapid expansion of the factory system absolutely necessary. But the British manufacturing interests are opposed to the development of modern industries in India, which is one of their principal markets. They have used, among other things, legislation to retard the growth of manufacturing industries in India, as seen in the foregoing pages. Legislation cannot serve the best interest of the workers by interfering with the growth of the factory system which opens to them new industrial opportunities.

INDEX.

Printed by Lande & Co., Berlin-Charlottenburg.

Bei Fragen zur Produktsicherheit wenden Sie sich bitte an:
If you have any questions regarding product safety,
please contact:

Walter de Gruyter GmbH
Genthiner Straße 13
10785 Berlin
productsafety@degruyterbrill.com